The School/Work Nexus:

Transition of Youth from School to Work

by

Eli Ginzberg

A Diamond Jubilee Publication of the

Phi Delta Kappa Educational Foundation

Cover design by Victoria Voelker

To

Florence and John Lawrence

Who were adopted into our family a half century ago; and who, in turn, adopted my mother, thereby adding greatly to the joy of her later years.

Publication of this monograph has been
financed in part through a generous
contribution from Paul Bohem as a
memorial to his late wife
Alice Bohem, educator.
Mr. Bohem is a member of the Mount Baldy
Chapter of Phi Delta Kappa in Claremont,
California.

Table of Contents

Preface

T his monograph has been prepared in response to an invitation from the Phi Delta Kappa Educational Foundation. The invitation suggested that "senior scholars share some of their wisdom gained from a lifelong career in their chosen field."

Accepting the invitation had its serendipitous consequences. It turned out that 1979 was the year during which the Carter Administration undertook a thorough review of its youth policies as prelude to new legislative proposals to Congress in 1980 when the 1977 Youth Act came up for reauthorization. As chairman of the National Commission for Employment Policy, the statutory body responsible for advising the President and Congress on a wide range of employment problems, I have had the advantage of participating in the Administration's review and in the extensive work carried out by the commission and its staff for its *Fifth Annual Report* submitted in December 1979, which focused on recommendations aimed at improving the employability of youth.

These are the policy concerns that have been present and dominant while this monograph was being written. My own career in research in human resources provides the foundation for the approach, the conceptions, and the conclusions reported in this monograph. For 40 years my colleagues and I at Columbia University have studied almost every facet of human resources. We have dealt at length with subjects directly relevant to the present inquiry, including occupational choice and career guidance, educational preparation and work performance, the preparation of minority youth for the world of work, military manpower, and the job problems of inner-city youth.

As a postscript since the presidential election in November, 1980, Congress did not act to reauthorize youth legislation because of a lack of agreement on funding, on a sub-minimum wage, and on the proposed appropriation for secondary education. Nevertheless, there is considerable support among senior Republican as well as Democratic legislators for a more effective federal program to assist disadvantaged youth in securing employment in the regular economy. It is possible, even likely, that new youth legislation will be introduced during the first or second year of the Reagan Administration

Although this monograph is sponsored by an educational organization, I must point out that my associates and I have never pursued research into the educational process: what transpires in the classroom between teacher and student; the factors that facilitate or retard mastery of reading and numbers; the antagonism and alienation that affects large numbers of students from low-income homes—these and related in-school problems and processes are not part of our capital. My views on these matters are drawn from the research of others; they do not reflect findings from our own investigations.

The point of this monograph is not to add one more research report to the never-ending stream of new publications dealing with detailed aspects of the educational system or of the labor market for youth. Rather, the objective is to set out the critical interfacing between these two large systems—the school and the world of work—with due regard for the way in which each is affected in turn by the family and the larger society. The point of this monograph is to help identify the reasons that the transition from school to work is relatively smooth for some young people and exceedingly difficult for others. In addition, we will assess the realistic options available to an affluent and concerned democracy for smoothing the path of those young people who are encountering major problems in making the transition.

Irving Greenberg, formerly Deputy Assistant Secretary for Manpower, U.S. Department of Defense, provided me with the background data on which Chapter 4 is based.

As many times previously, I owe much to the helpfulness of Sylvia Leef who transcribed my poor hand, to the careful checking of the statistical data by Anna Dutka, and to the pungent editing of Ruth S. Ginzberg.

Eli Ginzberg, Director
Conservation of Human Resources
Columbia University
December 1980

One:
Focus on Youth

Most Americans are addicted to the idea that anything that is real can be counted. Notwithstanding this predilection for statistics, the difficulties macroeconomists face in seeking to forecast the next turn in business activity and the problems encountered by criminologists who work with statistics should remind us of the fragile state of empirical social science. Another national trait is the denigration of historical evidence. We have always been future-oriented; the past is put out of sight and out of mind, since it may provide misleading cues and clues for a world that is experiencing rapid change.

But judgment, more than knowledge, depends on perspective, which, in turn, requires the evaluation of experience under different conditions and circumstances. This is the task of historical inquiry. It is true that we might draw the wrong inferences from history, but without the perspective that history contributes, we are certain to be disoriented.

With these stipulations, I will attempt to recapitulate the major developments on the American scene over the last 50 years to determine what light can be shed on the subject at hand—the transition of young people from school to work.

The late 1920s has been designated "The New Era" by those who believe that the last serious depression occurred in the 1890s and the United States subsequently entered upon a period of perpetual prosperity. I have no personal recollection of difficulties that either high school dropouts or graduates faced in finding a job during the Twenties. I do remember, however, the difficulty that some of my friends had in finding "good" openings, those with desirable working conditions where conscientious employees could look forward to advancement.

Youth unemployment became an issue of national concern during the devastating depression of the 1930s. Since the unemployment rates for male heads of households exceeded 25% in 1933 and never dropped below 10% throughout the decade, young people who wanted to join the labor force found it difficult to locate jobs. The federal government established the National Youth Administration to assist in-school and out-of-school youth with modest resources to obtain work and income. Later the government established the Civilian Conservation Corps, which enrolled a total of two and one-half million young men to work in the national parks and similar projects.

1

Because of the severity of adult unemployment in the 1930s, the trade unions lobbied with some success in the more industrialized states to raise the legal school-leaving age from 14 to 16 in the expectation that this would remove some of the competition for the large numbers of men who were still looking for work. Forty years later, during the recession of 1974-75, I was urged by trade union leaders in California to explore what new programs the National Commission for Manpower Policy might propose to delay young people from entering the labor market.

The screening of the male population in the U.S. for military service in World War II revealed several important defects in the educational preparation of the nation's youth. Although publicly supported education was established in the colonial period, at least in New England, and had been a recognized responsibility of localities and the states for the better part of a century, over 700,000 young men were rejected for military service because of "mental deficiency" (illiteracy); another 400,000 illiterates were accepted for service; and an additional 300,000 were considered borderline. In sum, almost one out of every 12 young men who registered for military service was illiterate (fifth-grade level) or had only borderline capacity to function at that level.

Several points are worth noting: the rejection rates for illiteracy were 10 times greater in the South than in the Far West; six times as many blacks were rejected as whites; the rejection rate for whites in the Southeast exceeded the rate for blacks in the Northeast and Far West.

In view of the recent (1960s and 1970s) efforts at remedial education, it is worth noting that during World War II the Army assigned 300,000 illiterates and slow learners to Special Training Units where, after eight to 12 weeks of instruction, 85% were found to be acceptable for service. In our follow-up study, we found that the true rate for unacceptables was quite low, 13%. While it is difficult for the Vietnam generation to understand it, during World War II most young men wanted to be in uniform, and those assigned to these Special Training Units were strongly motivated to reach an acceptable level of literacy so that they would not be discharged to civilian life at the end of their assignment.

World War II brought pervasive changes that have continued to influence youth employment up to the present. In 1940 four out of five blacks lived in the South, primarily in rural areas, where they worked the land as tenants or sharecroppers.

During and after the war blacks migrated from the farms to the cities, with the result that, on the average, blacks became more urbanized than whites. Blacks also migrated from the South to the North and West in such large numbers that today only one of every two blacks lives in the South.

The blacks, even those in the younger age group (25-29), who were heavily caught up in this mass migration were generally poorly educated. In 1940 more than one out of four was illiterate; only one in nine had completed high school. On the average young blacks had completed seven years of school; young whites had completed almost 10½ years. These figures do not reflect differences in the quality of the education, which, if taken into account, would reveal a still wider gap between blacks and whites.

Since much of the later analysis will focus on and around the differentially high rates of unemployment among minority youth, I wish to emphasize here that, because of statistical conventions, the blacks who lived on Southern farms prior to the large-scale migration were not counted as unemployed as long as they were engaged for some period of the year in working the land on which they lived or were hired by somebody else. They may have worked less than 100 days a year and have earned very little, but according to the statistical convention, they were *underemployed*, not *unemployed*. We must be careful, therefore, in assessing the current situation of many urban black youth; we must not see their present plight as unequivocally worse than the conditions experienced by their fathers and grandfathers who lived and worked in Southern agriculture. The estimated annual income of a Southern black farm family in 1940 was under $500!

At the end of World War II, most economists believed that the nation was certain to confront a serious unemployment problem as a result of the approaching demobilization of some 10,000,000 servicemen and women and of the major dislocations that would attend the conversion from military to consumer output. The dominant view held that the nation would experience rates of unemployment in the same range as in the depressed 1930s. Fortunately this expectation proved unfounded: the pent-up demand for consumer goods, the alacrity with which businessmen were able to reconvert to a peace-time basis, the voluntary withdrawal of large numbers of women from the work force, the GI benefits that steered large numbers of veterans into school or training courses all contributed to the successful transition.

I have recently checked the principal publications prepared for and emanating from the 1960 White House Conference on Children and Youth, and the subject of youth unemployment, including the unemployment of black youth, was conspicuously absent. In a major address to the conference titled "Negro Youth on Democracy's Growing Edge," Frederick D. Patterson said, "The ability of minorities to get jobs . . . is probably the most crucial and pragmatic single test of progress . . . What are the prospects for minority youth? The decade of 1950-60 has been one of comparatively full employment." While Patterson was taking a favorable reading on the employment outlook for black youth, the U.S. Department of Labor issued its manpower outlook for the 1960s, noting future major changes in the labor market; specifically, the proximate increase in the number of young entrants into the labor force as a consequence of the steep rise in the birth rate in the immediate post-war period.

Before the end of the decade of the Sixties, over 4,000,000 young people would annually reach the age of 18, up from about 2,000,000 in the 1950s, a reflection of the low birth rates of the depressed 1930s. The manpower specialists in the U.S. Department of Labor, as well as observers outside of government, were increasingly concerned in the early 1960s with the fact that after each of the last three recessions—in 1948-49, 1958-59, and 1961-62—the country had a higher level of unemployment. This, together with the large increases in young workers and the substantial numbers of women entering or returning to the labor force, pointed to serious unemployment in the years ahead.

The Kennedy Administration, with broad-based support from the Republicans, passed the Manpower Development and Training Act (MDTA) in 1962 to alleviate one aspect of the employment problem. The initial thrust of MDTA was to assist skilled workers, who had lost their jobs because of automation, to find alternative employment after participating in a federally-supported training or retraining program.

It was not until 1964 that Congress directed its attention specifically to helping young people in search of employment. Although Senator Hubert Humphrey had sought congressional approval for a broad-based program for youth, he had to settle for considerably less: the Job Corps, for young persons who had few salable skills for the employment marketplace, and the Neighborhood Youth Corps, a summer program for young people in the cities.

Despite the sustained expansion of the economy that started in 1961 and ended in 1969, which set a record for years without a recession, and despite the additional demand for youth by the Armed Forces to meet the escalating requirements of our deepening involvement in Vietnam, considerable numbers of young people, especially minority youth, could not find regular jobs. But it was not until the recession of 1970, which the Nixon Administration mistakenly thought would draw the inflationary virus out of the U.S. economy, that youth unemployment in general and the unemployment of black youth in particular began to attract attention.

When the Twentieth Century Fund inquired in 1970 whether I would head a task force on black youth unemployment, I asked for a few days in which to review the data before making a commitment to undertake the assignment. I knew that the black population had made significant gains in employment, occupational mobility, and income during the 1960s and, until I looked closely at the figures, I was unaware that these seemingly favorable trends had not been sufficiently pervasive to assure a job for all black young people who reached working age. In fact, I was appalled at what my summary review of the figures revealed. Our report in 1971 carried the title, *The Job Crisis for Black Youth.*

Although the Comprehensive Employment and Training Act (CETA) was passed in December 1973, and was substantially broadened the following year to help check the ravages of the recession and further amended in 1976, it was not until March 1977 that Congress passed manpower legislation aimed specifically at improving the employability and employment of youth.

In setting the stage for a review of the rites of passage between school and work, we must also pay brief attention to the major transformations in the educational system that accompanied the labor market transformations and the new federal programs designed to improve the prospects of groups experiencing difficulties in finding and holding jobs.

School systems, many of which had been hurt by the long depression of the 1930s, benefitted greatly from a new infusion of public funds in the post-World War II period. Urban and suburban taxpayers became willing and able to support a much higher level of public expenditure. New school buildings, better prepared teachers, more ancillary services (from counseling to driver education), the spectacular expansion of community colleges and branches of state universities in urban centers, additional funds for vocational and technical training, and, after 1965, special federal funding to improve the educational opportunities for youngsters from low-income families—all this and more occurred in the Fifties, Sixties, and early Seventies. While much of the new money went to accommodate the vastly increased student population, the increases on a per capita basis, inflationary distortions eliminated, amounted to well over 100% between 1950 and 1970.

Dollar flows were important and so was the decision of the U.S. Supreme Court in 1954 that outlawed school segregation. However slowly this decision has been implemented, it has enabled a significant number of black youngsters in the South to attend schools with white classmates and white teachers. In the North, the exodus of middle-class white families to the suburbs left more and more inner-city schools catering exclusively to minority groups.

In the early Sixties, James Conant warned about the dangers of concentrating exclusively on school desegregation and to miss in that preoccupation two parallel challenges confronting American democracy: 1) how to assure that the large number of youths who, in spite of desegregation, would continue to attend segregated schools in the slums for a long time to come could be more effectively educated, and 2) how our society could assure that these young people could obtain jobs when they were ready to work.

Conant found American society oblivious to the "social dynamite" inherent in the inadequate education and the large-scale unemployment of ghetto youth and warned that if the country failed to act, it would pay a high price. An adequate response to this warning is yet to come.

It is not easy to explain why the American people have been so slow to focus on the school/work nexus, but if this introductory chapter is to provide perspective, we must consider the issue and advance some interpretations.

It is my view that, until recently, the recognition of youth unemployment as a problem has been simply denied. At a meeting of consultants to the National Institute of Education in the early 1970s, Theodore Schultz, one of the founders of the Chicago school of human capital, became quite impatient with me because of my emphasis on this issue. He commented sharply, "You know what happens to unemployed youth— when they reach their twenties, they get jobs." My not-so-respectful reply was to the effect that that might be true for those who, in the interim, had not been killed, committed suicide, or been locked up in prison.

In 1967 President Johnson appointed a "secret" White House Task Force to advise him on the problems of the inner city. It was secret because the President wanted to keep his options open in the event that he decided not to go forward with the recommendations of the Task Force, and this, in fact, turned out to be the case. Chaired by George Shultz, who was at that time dean of the University of Chicago School of Business, and with broad representation from business, labor, academic, minority groups, and government, the Task Force unanimously recommended, among other things, the establishment of an experimental school system from nursery through high school and independent of the educational establishment. The Task Force had hopes of determining whether such a freestanding school, uninhibited by the barnacles of bureaucracy, could successfully educate youngsters from low-income families living in the ghetto. The total cost of the Task Force's innovative programs amounted to between 14 and 18 billion dollars, a sum that was ruled out of bounds because of the mounting expenditures for Vietnam.

Unwilling to ask Congress for large new programs that he knew it would not approve, President Johnson instead sought in 1967-68 to elicit the cooperation of leaders in the business community to facilitate hiring the hard-to-employ. Henry Ford II and the other leaders who responded obviously were sensitive to the problem, having witnessed the conflagrations set off by urban rioters who put the torch to homes, offices, and community facilities as an expression of their frustrations.

Several years later, after having placed several hundred thousand hard-to-employ persons on their payrolls, most employers discovered that few were still working for them. Turnover is always high among new workers, and it is especially high if the new workers face transportation problems in getting to work and if their supervisors tend to be hostile because of racial prejudice. In addition to the losses from these causes, the recession severed many of the remaining new employees from the payroll because of their low seniority. From the end of the 1960s to the end of the 1970s, American business has been loath to experiment anew in hiring the hard-to-employ. It may turn out that the reorganization of the National Alliance of Business in 1978 and the funding of Title VII of CETA, Private Industry Councils, will reverse the long-term noninvolvement of the business sector.

7

Because economists have preempted the field of employment, including explorations of unemployment, the concluding section of this chapter will look more closely at the dominant economic theories of employment, some of which complement and some of which contradict each other.

The following theories run the gamut from denying that youth unemployment is a problem worthy of public attention to a view that, while it may be a serious problem, not much can be done about it since it is embedded in 18 or more years of cumulative developmental deficits. In brief, here are the theories:

1. Much of the reported unemployment among youth is "voluntary" in that it reflects young persons quitting rather than losing jobs, a process connected with their explorations of the labor market prior to settling down. This interpretation gains support from the finding that the average span of unemployment among youth is shorter than among older workers. Further support for the "voluntary" nature of youth unemployment is the joint explanations that point to "the loss of the work ethic" and the availability of alternative sources of income for those who don't work (primarily from welfare or from illicit activities). The protagonists hold that teenage mothers, who are unmarried or whose husbands have left or divorced them, receive sufficiently high welfare payments in money and in kind to deter them from looking for paid employment. The explanation for young unemployed men is that many can make more money in a few hours spent "hustling" than in a week of delivering parcels or washing dishes. Consequently, many who are counted as unemployed or out of the labor force are in fact "working" outside the regular economy, usually less than full time.

2. Another theory accepts the reality of high youth unemployment but finds the root of the problem in the malfunctioning of employment markets. Policy makers in the 1970s were unwilling to run the economy at or even close to the full employment level. Accordingly, the chronic weakness in demand means that some job seekers will not find jobs and young people, most of whom lack experience and skill, are among the most likely victims of this policy.

3. The foregoing explanation is popular among the left-of-center economists, while those to the right-of-center see high youth unemployment closely linked to the continuing rise in the minimum wage, together with its broadened coverage. Employers avoid hiring young inexperienced persons

because the wage they must pay them is significantly greater than their prospective productivity. If employers could pay them less, they would hire more young people. Although this is true, I want to be counted with those economists who question whether a special minimum wage for youth would be desirable. The arguments against it are substantial and include: the long-term commitment of the U.S. to pay according to the work, not according to the characteristics of the worker; the dangers of substituting younger for older workers, thereby reducing the total social benefit; the attitude of many ghetto youth that keeps them from accepting employment, even at the minimum wage, if the job appears to be dead-end; the recent availability of targeted tax credits that provide substantial financial assistance to employers if they hire disadvantaged youth.

4. Another theory holds that high youth unemployment results from the geographic gap between where young people live and where entry-level jobs are expanding. High youth unemployment is characteristic of inner-city and low-income rural areas. Job expansion, particularly in manufacturing, is occurring in the suburbs and recently in selected communities in the Sunbelt. Both of these localities are beyond the reach of many young inner-city job seekers.

5. Another explanation for the job difficulties of young people stresses the competition they face from the continuing flow of mature women into the labor market whenever jobs become available. Since many of these women are better educated and more stable than minority youth who drop out or get pushed out of school without having acquired a diploma, they are preferred by employers. Minority youth are also seen by some researchers to be vulnerable to the competition of the large numbers of immigrants, legal and undocumented, who have been entering the U.S. in substantial numbers over the last decade. These newcomers, particularly those who are not legally permitted to work, are eager to take any type of job that is open and to work hard, usually for minimum wages. Their availability precludes the necessity of employers improving their work environment and wages, which, if improved, might attract a substantial number of unemployed minority youth.

6. Discrimination based on race, ethnic origin, or sex extends into every aspect of our society. While experts differ in the weight they attach to discrimination in handicapping minority youth in their search for desirable employment, I hold with

those who see it as highly damaging. Employers differ in their policies of hiring minorities, and some are under pressure to increase the proportion of minority workers on their payrolls. Still, the practices followed by the personnel departments of large organizations are often passively if not actively hostile toward minorities, especially those whose dress, speech, and manner differ markedly from the norm. We know that in the absence of alternative sources of labor supply, even highly prejudiced employers will alter their hiring practices and accept minorities. But, as we have seen, most employers in recent years have been able to choose employees from a large and diverse labor market.

7. A final explanation of high youth unemployment can be subsumed under the heading of "inadequate human capital." Many youths, especially minority youths, are unemployed because they lack the minimal competencies, work orientation, and behavioral traits that are essential for finding and holding regular jobs. The protagonists of this theory point to the large numbers of minority youth who fail to graduate from high school and the substantial proportion among them who lack the minimum skills of reading, writing, and computation that most jobs now require. And these defects, serious as they are, are not the total of their handicaps. These theorists emphasize that many young people are unable or unwilling to accept the discipline, authority, and restraints that are inherent in jobs. Workers who are unable to get to work regularly and on time, who decide to take a day off when they feel like it, who respond to direction and criticism from their supervisors by becoming surly or hostile, who get into conflicts with their fellow employees—these workers will not survive long on the job.

There is no way to choose among these conflicting or complementary explanations of why so many minority youth are having such difficulties in getting a toehold in the world of work. Other explanations by respected scholars should at least be noted. These include the unrealistic expectations that many young people have about jobs and careers; their reluctance to accept certain kinds of work (such as domestic service or other service employment); their alienation from society, which leads to their turning their backs on any type of regular employment; or their conviction that "the system" will not pay off for them any more than it has paid off for their parents.

Analysis of these alternative theories must await our review of the interaction among the family, the school, the U.S. Armed Forces, and the labor market, each of which influences the job and career prospects of young people. Only at the end of such an analysis will we have developed a reasonable basis for public intervention.

Two:
Of Concepts and Numbers

D espite disturbingly high rates of youth unemployment throughout most of the 1960s and 1970s, it was not until 1977 that Congress focused on the issue and sought to intervene. While we have sufficient data to frame the youth unemployment problem and to assess its impact, there are gaps in our knowledge about the critical years after young people stop attending school and move into the world of work, either directly or after a number of detours.

In this chapter I shall outline the contours of youth employment and unemployment on the basis of data compiled by the federal government. However, it is first necessary to assess the categories used in collecting the data so that the potential as well as the limitations of the available information can be appraised.

Let us first consider the lower and upper age boundaries of the term "youth." Some years ago the U.S. Departments of Commerce and Labor raised the lower age level from 14 to 16 in recognition of the fact that most young people remain on the school rolls until at least 16. In some states the school-leaving age is 17 or 18 or until a student has acquired a high school diploma. A new pattern may be emerging: in California young people may leave school at any time after their sixteenth birthday if they can demonstrate through an examination that they have basic competencies in reading, writing, and mathematics and some general knowledge and ability to use these competencies in problem solving.

The National Commission on Employment and Unemployment Statistics, which submitted its recommendations to Congress in the fall of 1979 on the basis of its comprehensive review of the quantity and quality of labor force data, considered recommending that the lower age level be raised from 16 to 18 on the ground that more young people remain in school than leave prior to the age of 18. It finally decided against this recommendation because, it felt, it is important to be able to monitor the employment experience of young people who enter the work force at 16.

The Commission's decision to recommend continuing to use the age of 16 as the lower age level for estimating the labor force does not mean, however, that there are no problems connected with the decision. Many 14- and 15-year-olds who are still in school seek or hold part-time and summer jobs, and some participate in work-study programs. Both Congress and the federal departments involved in overseeing various training and employment programs have been under conflicting pressures to treat this younger group in different ways. Since there are insufficient appropriations to cover all potential claimants for employability services, Congress has excluded the 14- and 15-year-olds from many employment and training programs. On the other hand, to exclude them from participating could deprive those who need work opportunities to help their families and to help keep them on the school rolls.

Government agencies usually divide the youth population into two categories: teenagers (those between 16 and 19) and young people aged 20 to 24. Some analysts prefer to divide youth into teenagers and those aged 20 to 21 on the assumption that the definition of youth should not be extended beyond 21, but most governmental reporting systems do not recognize this lower cut-off point. It should be noted that many states provide that when a young person reaches 18, he or she becomes an adult in the legal sense of the term. But incongruities remain: most 18-year-olds continue to live in their parents' homes or are supported by them if they live away from home; they are permitted to vote in federal and many state elections; they may control their property. Nevertheless their experiences in the labor market continue to differ substantially from those in their mid- and later twenties.

For the purpose of labor market analysis, then, youth is usually defined as young people between the ages of 16 and 24, but with special focus on those between 16 and 19 years of age. What measures should be used to judge how well or how poorly those who stop their education make the transition from school to work?

Every summer millions of young people, most of whom plan to return to school in the fall, seek either full- or part-time jobs to earn money, keep busy, gain some work experience, or explore the adult world. Many young people do find jobs, usually with the help of relatives or friends. But many others do not. Since 1964 Congress has appropriated a sizable sum every year to provide approximately 1,000,000 summer jobs for youngsters from low-income homes who might otherwise be on the streets and getting into trouble. In 1978 approximately $750 million was appropriated for this purpose. A Government Accounting Office (GAO) report in February 1979 was highly critical of the Summer Youth Employment Development

Program, on the ground that the work experience offered by this program was deficient. In my opinion, however, the government auditors underestimated the extent to which Congress considered this program more a method of income transfer than one of training; it assumes that young people with money in their pockets are less likely to cause disturbances in the urban centers.

Many youngsters who work in the summer also want part-time jobs during the school year. Some obtain as much part-time work as they want; others are less successful. Because of the age groupings into which our labor force data are subdivided, no sharp distinction is made between the unemployment of a young man in his early twenties who is the head of a household and has a wife and child to support and the high school student living at home in a middle-income family who lost a babysitting position.

On the basis of the available data, we can distinguish the employment of in-school from that of out-of-school youth; further we can distinguish between full-time and part-time employment. It is less easy to differentiate the household arrangements and income needs of young persons who are reported or who report themselves as unemployed. Some youngsters are on their own and must support themselves; others live at home and receive allowances from their parents; still others live at home, but the family income is marginal and the young persons need to contribute to family support or at least to obtain their own spending money.

In an ideal world in which the goals of the Humphrey-Hawkins Full Employment and Balanced Economic Growth Act were fully implemented, there would be part-time or full-time jobs for all young persons depending on their desires and needs, subject only to some societal determination of the minimum age at which a young person could leave school and work full time. Since we are a considerable distance from achieving this goal, Congress must continue to stipulate the criteria of age and family income that permit young people to participate in federal training and employment programs.

In our search for perspective on youth employment and unemployment, we must go beyond the considerations of age span, distinctions between in-school and out-of-school youth, between youths seeking full-time and youths seeking part-time work, and the economic circumstances of their families. These are important considerations, but they cannot provide a comprehensive view of youth in the U.S. labor market today. We also need to review major developments over the past quarter century so that we can increase our knowledge of the much larger numbers of young people who want jobs, the extent to which employers have been able to accommodate them, whether those who have not found jobs are heavily concentrated among certain groups, and the alternatives open to young people who do not find jobs or who become so discouraged that they stop looking.

The unemployment rate has become the most important single measure of the quality of performance of the American economy. Therefore, any pronounced rise in the unemployment rate for young people, as did in fact occur between the mid-1950s and the mid-1970s when the rate for white teenagers rose from about 10% to about 17% and for black teenagers from 16% to 38%, must be taken as evidence of the malperformance of the economy, particularly in providing employment opportunities for young people. During this same period the unemployment rate among the 20- to 24-year-olds increased from approximately 4.5% to 12%.

These data underscore the increasing difficulty young people faced over these two decades in finding jobs, but they do not tell the whole story. At least two additional criteria must be considered: What happened to the total rate of employment of youth and what was the experience of different groups in obtaining jobs?

As we have noted, the number of young people reaching working age (16) does not remain the same from one decade to the next. The numbers of those aged 18 to 24 remained relatively stable between 1950 and 1960 and then advanced steeply by 1977.

Young People in the United States, 1950-1977
(in millions)

Year	Total	14-17	18-21	22-24
1950	24.5	8.4	9.0	7.1
1960	26.8	11.2	9.2	6.4
1977	45.2	16.8	16.8	11.6

While the U.S. population increased from 180 to 216 million (20% increase) between 1960 and 1977, the number of young people aged 14 to 24 increased by about 70%. In fact the young people accounted for one out of every two persons added to the total population.

Of Concepts and Numbers

In the 13 years between 1947 and 1960 there was no difference in the number of young people aged 16 to 24 in the civilian labor force; in both years this age group accounted for approximately 11.5 million. In fact, since the total labor force grew by about 15% over this period, the proportion of young people employed or looking for jobs declined. But the numbers and labor force status of young people changed radically between 1960 and 1977. The total number of young people in the labor force more than doubled during this period; it increased from 11.5 to 23.7 million. It is striking to note the increase in the number of employed young people in the labor force: the number was 10.2 million in 1960 and 20.4 million in 1977. Since total employment increased from 66 to 91 million (slightly under 40%) in these same years, the absorption of over 10 million young workers was notable on two counts: they accounted for one out of every 2.5 additional workers and their rate of employment growth was two-and-a-half times as rapid as for the labor force as a whole.

It makes little sense to argue, as many do, that the U.S. economy is fundamentally hostile to young people. The foregoing data suffice to rule that out. These figures lend support to those who believe that youth unemployment has not been, and is not at present, a serious economic or social problem; the labor market has shown considerable flexibility in accommodating the vastly enlarged number of young people ready to work.

Another way to assess the labor market is to consider the unemployment of young people, in numbers and percentages, as more of them sought jobs after 1960. In 1960 there were 1.3 million young people between the ages of 16 and 24 out of work, roughly 11% of the age group. In 1977 the numbers out of work exceeded 3.2 million, somewhat less than 14% of the age group.

To understand the unemployment data in terms of both what they reveal and what they conceal, we must realize that a person over 16 years of age is counted as unemployed only if he, or a member of the household in which he lives, reports that he has been actively looking for work but has not found a job. What of those who have no job, have not started to look, or have ceased looking because they have concluded that there are no openings for them? These young people are not considered unemployed; they are considered out of the labor force because they are not actively looking for jobs. The preferred way to develop a more inclusive measure of manpower utilization and underutilization is to consider the proportion of the total age group that is employed.

In his insightful paper written for the American Assembly in August 1979, Richard B. Freeman of Harvard University provides the relevant data by race and sex. With respect to white males he found that between 1964 and 1977 there were substantial gains in the percentage who held jobs:

Percent Young White Males Employed, 1964, 1977

Age	1964	1977
16-17	36.5	44.3
18-19	57.7	65.2
20-24	79.3	80.5

Among white females the gains were even greater:

Percent Young White Females Employed, 1964, 1977

Age	1964	1977
16-17	25.3	37.5
18-19	43.0	54.3
20-24	45.3	61.4

These data provide supporting evidence for those who believe that, despite the larger numbers of unemployed and rising rate of unemployment, more young people were able to find jobs in 1977 than in 1964. At a time when a much larger number of white young people were reaching working age, the labor market was able to provide substantially more opportunities for them, even though some were not able to make an easy transition.

What about the blacks? The figures for young black men are disheartening:

Percent Young Black Males Employed, 1964, 1977

Age	1964	1977
16-17	27.6	18.0
18-19	51.8	36.0
20-24	78.1	61.2

Among young black women, there was relatively little change over these years:

Percent Young Black Females Employed, 1964, 1977

Age	1964	1977
16-17	12.5	12.5
18-19	32.9	28.0
20-24	43.7	45.4

The percentage of young black men and women who succeeded in their search for employment in 1977 was lower than the relative percentage who succeeded in 1964. When their experience is compared to that of their white peers, their handicaps are highlighted.

Among the 16- and 17-year-olds, the percentage of white males holding jobs in 1977 was almost two-and-a-half times that of blacks. Among the same age group, the discrepancy between white and black females is even greater; the ratio is three to one. Even when we consider young adults, there is a marked difference in favor of the whites, male and female.

The different experiences of young blacks and whites in the labor market can be rounded out by considering a brief overview of their respective unemployment rates, especially from the mid-Fifties to the late Seventies. In the mid-Fifties the white unemployment rate for teenagers fluctuated around 10%. In the mid-Sixties the white rate had risen little more than one percentage point; the black rate by 10 points. By 1977 the white rate had dropped from its peak of about 18% in 1975 to 15.4%, but the black rate kept moving up to over 38%. These figures demonstrate that the unemployment rate among white teenagers increased by half over the 10% figure in the mid-1950s; the black rate skyrocketed from 16% to over 38%, an increase of about 140%.

So far, we have focused exclusively on the adaptive capacity of the labor market to create part-time or full-time jobs for the vastly increased numbers of young people who became available for work after the early 1960s. Now we must consider the ages at which young people leave school so that we can determine whether changes in this pattern influenced the numbers and the time that young people enter the labor market. Richard B. Freeman has again prepared a most useful table:

Patterns of School Enrollment Among
Young White Males by Percent

Year	16-17	18-19	20-24
1964	90.4	52.4	25.6
1969	92.2	60.9	33.2
1977	89.5	47.7	25.7

Patterns of School Enrollment Among
Young Black Males by Percent

Year	16-17	18-19	20-24
1964	84.3	39.9	8.3
1969	87.4	49.5	20.5
1977	92.5	50.6	26.1

Several points are noteworthy. Among white males the percentage of each age group enrolled in school rose between 1964 and 1969 but dropped thereafter. The decline in the two older groups between 1969 and 1977 is striking. One reason for the decline might have been that, with the cessation of hostilities in Vietnam, men no longer had to stay in school to avoid the draft. Another reason might have been the steep rise in college tuition and the new uncertainties about whether a college degree would "pay off" in terms of improved job and career prospects, especially for those with only moderate intellectual capacity and interest.

The trends in black enrollment are equally striking and very heartening. The largest percentage gain was achieved by blacks in their early twenties, whose school enrollment increased more than threefold from 1964 to 1977. In 1977 the percentage of blacks in each age group enrolled in school exceeded that of their white peers, a social statistic that is astonishing since considerations of family income and parental education weigh so heavily in favor of the whites. We must also consider to what extent blacks who cannot find jobs decide to remain in or return to school in the hope of improving their employability.

The steep increases in the school enrollment of blacks in their teens and early twenties would have reduced their availability for full-time work but not necessarily for part-time jobs. Since so many come from families whose income is modest at best and often close to the poverty level, these students need to earn part or all of their expenses. Nevertheless, the sharp decline in the percentage of young blacks who are working cannot be accounted for, except to a minor degree, by the substantial rise in school enrollments.

Although we will defer consideration of such important matters as wage rates, earnings, career opportunities, and other important aspects of the jobs that young people obtain, we are now in a position to draw some tentative conclusions about the performance of the American economy in providing employment opportunities for young people as they enter the world of work.

Of Concepts and Numbers

1. The U.S. does not face a crisis in youth unemployment. Although both the number and percentage of young people who want jobs and can't find them is greater than a decade or two ago, it is also true that many more youths, both in absolute numbers and as a proportion of their age group, are currently at work. The economy has shown great capacity to absorb them.

2. This positive reading about jobs for young people does not imply that the work opportunities during the summer and the school year are sufficient for meeting the desires and the needs of all young people, including those who are 14 or 15 years old, for work experience and for spending money. But this failure, while it may be more dysfunctional than the public realizes, does not constitute a crisis.

3. A crisis does exist among black youth. This is revealed by their low labor force participation, low employment, and high unemployment, both among males and females. Fortunately, not all blacks find it difficult to make the transition from school to work, but the data we have reviewed indicate that the process is much more difficult for blacks than for whites.

Since blacks account for only about 11% of the population and since most of them are employed, why do we call their circumstances a crisis? The answer is that the majority of black teenagers are out of work or out of the labor force. Moreover, if we take account of the second largest minority group, Hispanics, who may supplant blacks as our largest minority by the 1990's, the problem takes on heightened importance.

Further reason to confront the crisis rather than ignore it is that blacks and Hispanics will account for more than their proportionate share (based on their present population) of the young people who will reach working age in the 1980s. Instead of accounting for about one out of every seven youths of working age by the end of the 1980s, the ratio will be closer to two out of seven.

If the above figure is not sufficiently convincing, we can add that in many regions of the country and in many of the nation's leading cities—New York, Washington, Atlanta, Los Angeles, Houston, and Chicago—minority youth will account for the majority of the new entrants into the work force.

Finally, ours is a pluralistic economy and society. The U.S. cannot retain a leadership position in the world unless it can assure its domestic tranquility and develop and utilize its human resources effectively. It will not be able to accomplish this goal unless it provides opportunities for work and participation to its minority youth.

Three:
The Shaping Institutions

M ost young people make the transition from school to a
job with relatively little difficulty unless the local or the
national economies are in the doldrums and older, more
experienced workers are being laid off.

With little or no job experience other than occasional part-
time work or summer employment, the early months, even the
first years after school, are a time of search and exploration of
the realities of the job world for young people. There is no
effective substitute for this period of exploration. Visits to
plants, participation in counseling sessions, even enrolling in
a vocational training program can help introduce young people to some of the realities of the work place, but they cannot
take the place of hands-on work experience.

The combination of no prior work experience and few skills
makes many employers reluctant to hire young people. This
reluctance is increased when employers realize that many
young people are likely to leave jobs within the first few weeks
or months, because they are either dissatisfied with the work
or because they are searching for jobs that suit them better.

One of the theories popular with conservative economists
to explain the high unemployment among teenagers is based
on their behavioral traits. The theory holds that their unemployment is primarily voluntary because they change jobs
so frequently. As with most simplistic explanations, this
theory has some basis in fact. Other simplistic theories run
the gamut from the minimum wage law, which employers feel
forces them to pay young people more than they contribute and
therefore they are reluctant to hire them, to the hypothesis that
since a disproportionate number of unemployed teenagers are
black, racial discrimination must be the dominant cause of
their difficulties in getting and holding jobs.

These sweeping generalizations based on behavioral traits,
the minimum wage, or racial discrimination go further than
the available data will support and lack depth. Except through
some generalized proxy variable such as educational achievement, they take no account of the cumulative experiences of
the young person or of how these experiences have shaped how
the person thinks, acts, and will react once he or she starts
to look for a job.

The thrust of this chapter is that what happens during the
transition from school to work cannot be understood and,

22

therefore, cannot be subject to effective social interventions until we delineate the developmental process through which students have passed and identify some of the difficulties facing them when they enter the job market. Let us then consider the interactions among family, school, community, and society that, through mutual reinforcement, transform children into adults.

The scholarly community is not in agreement about the shaping role of any one of these institutions, and there is even less consensus about the dynamics of their interactions. I will attempt to avoid basing any part of the following analysis on extreme formulations. I will also attempt to alert the reader to the tentative nature of some of the assumptions underlying the formulations guiding the analysis. While experts may disagree on the importance they assign to the family as the principal nurturing institution, there is broad agreement among all of them, from anthropologists and psychologists to sociologists and economists, that what happens to a person is greatly influenced by the circumstances of the family into which he or she is born. I have often told my students that the most important decision in their lives is their choice of parents!

Fortunately, most children in the U.S. are born to parents who want them, who have sufficient income to provide the essentials for normal growth, and who can provide a supportive emotional environment for their children.

While this pattern is the norm, the deviations from it are considerable. First, many children are born into families in which there is only one parent. Many others do not live with both of their natural parents. When Daniel Patrick Moynihan, then the Assistant Secretary of Labor, became aware in the mid-1960s that approximately half of all black children reach 18 without having lived with both of their natural parents, he believed that he had found the key to the desperate circumstances of the black family. As he saw it, this was the cause of the low income, low occupational status, high crime rates, high rates of rejection for military service, high crime stigma of disadvantage that characterize a larger proportion of blacks. He stressed the fact that the absence of a man in so many black households was the direct cause of the family being on welfare, of children growing up without adequate discipline, of children never acquiring an understanding of and expectation to participate in the world of work.

With the benefit of hindsight we can better appreciate both the strengths and weaknesses of the Moynihan Report.

Moynihan's presentation appeared to place the blame on the victimized party. Furthermore, the report gave the impression that not much progress could be expected until blacks "pulled themselves together" and began to behave like the white majority in establishing and maintaining a normal family structure in which two parents share responsibility for raising their offspring. The report was deficient in that it did not make the connection between the second-class status of black males in U.S. society and their behavior as providers. Nor did it present the extent to which the black community had for generations relied on the extended family, especially the female relatives, to provide alternatives to the vulnerable male as spouse and supporter.

⋇ Nevertheless, these defects in analysis and presumptions should not obscure the importance of the link between family status and the fate of young people that Moynihan recognized. Children reared by only one parent have several disadvantages: a single parent is often unable to cope with all the demands on him or her; low family income translates into less of everything from food to toys; the infant and the young child are less likely to receive the stimulation needed for affective and cognitive development. Other possible deficits range from the low self-esteem of families on welfare to the difficulties that children in such homes have in developing a knowledge of the world beyond their immediate environs.

Kenneth Keniston and his colleagues published in 1977 a wide-ranging analysis of the ways in which vulnerable families, that is, those at the lower end of the income distribution, those who belong to minority groups, and those with single heads of households, are handicapped in their attempts to provide their offspring with a reasonable start in life. Although Keniston's analysis could be criticized for its repeated emphasis on the dysfunctional correlates of low family income, the weight of the evidence that vulnerable families produce an excessive number of vulnerable children and young adults is compelling.

Developmental psychologists such as Benjamin Bloom have presented evidence that the amount of stimulation that a child receives up to the age of 4—some investigators place even greater emphasis on the first two years of life—greatly affects his later learning capabilities. Therefore, developmental psychologists content that mothers who do not interact with their offspring verbally and through other modes of expression contribute to the atrophy of the child's potential to master language and cognitive skills. This school of thought sees the intellectual and emotional understimulation of youngsters in low-income families, especially those in one-parent households, as a primary cause in the difficulties that many experience when they enter the first grade.

A major remedial effort was introduced during the Great Society days (mid-1960s) called Head Start, a pre-school program aimed at providing children from low-income families with an early stimulating learning environment. The aim underlying this social experiment was to "compensate" for the shortcomings in these youngsters' home environments so that they would be more nearly equal to other children when they began their formal education.

While the effort did have some positive impacts, including better health and nutrition for these children, the evaluations with respect to the children's learning potential were equivocal. On balance, they suggest that unless reinforcement is continued after the child enters the first grade, the improvement in test scores that results from participating in Head Start is not maintained.

The child's learning potential and the extent to which it is influenced by his or her family's circumstances appear more complex than the developmental psychologists believe. Even if we disregard extremists such as Arthur Jensen, who holds that there are genetic reasons why black children do not achieve as well in school as their white peers, the effect of the environment warrants probing. Consider the following: black children learn very early that they belong to an inferior caste; that whites are hostile to them; and that no matter how hard they seek to conform and excel, they will be cheated of their just rewards as were their parents and grandparents.

To compound matters, race and class disabilities reinforce each other for the ghetto child. By the age of 3 or 4 disadvantaged children are streetwise. There is a wall between them and the occasional white who enters their world—the police officer, the visiting nurse, the physician, the kindergarten teacher. The "jiving syndrome," which defines the world of the streetwise youngster, has its own language, thought patterns, values, and goals.

Ghetto youngsters are thrown into contact with many older children and adults and learn as many new and different things as suburban middle-class white youngsters under the close supervision of their parents. But the white youngsters learn how to respond to adults and, thus, how to respond to the school curriculum; the ghetto youngsters have difficulty sitting still in class and have difficulty understanding the language and behavior of the teacher; they often feel that the teacher has little regard for them.

The educational establishment holds that many black youngsters do poorly in school because their parents do not encourage them to consider school as an opportunity, to be responsive to their teachers, to do their homework, to read on their own initiative. However, when educators receive the resources with which to perform their duties, they make an explicit commitment to the taxpayers to instruct all of the children, not just some of them, to an acceptable level of competence. Nevertheless, the performance of the large city school systems in this country is a source of despair for everybody—the educational leadership, the teaching staffs, the legislators, the parents of the children, and the children themselves.

There is no need here to sort out the claims and counterclaims among the concerned groups about how the responsibility for the shortfall in educational achievement should be apportioned. The critical point is that the shortfall has occurred and continues to exist and that it adds a burden to the later occupational adjustment of many ghetto youths.

A few pieces of evidence will establish the linkage between inadequate skill acquisition in school and later failure in the labor market. Using the experience of the armed forces in World War I, employers have increasingly utilized educational achievement as a screening device for initial hiring. They base their evaluation on test scores correlated with the mastery of school work as represented by diplomas or certificates. As Melvin Reder has so clearly demonstrated, the reason for the increased use of tests is not snobbism, discrimination, or rank foolishness on the part of employers, although each of these factors may play a part. During the Great Depression of the 1930s, R.H. Macy and Co. in New York City selected its sales force on the basis of educational achievement and discovered that a person with a master's degree was not necessarily better at dealing with bargain-seeking customers than was a high school dropout or graduate. Ivar Berg, in his challenging monograph, *Education and Jobs: The Great Training Robbery* (Praeger, 1970), hammered this point home by skillfully piecing together statistical data on workers' education relative to their productivity and overall performance.

In an economy in which most large and many small employers have become accustomed to using the high school diploma as an initial screening device for potential employees, people who do not have one—or its equivalent, the GED—are clearly at a disadvantage. To make matters worse, many large city school systems in the recent past—and some still follow the practice—awarded diplomas to young people who performed far below the expected levels of competence. These students were advanced from one grade to the next without having to demonstrate that they had acquired the knowledge and skills to justify promotion.

The poor performance of many large city schools goes beyond their failing to bring many students to the minimum level of competence needed to perform effectively as citizens and workers. The tensions in the classrooms, in the corridors, in the school yard and in the neighboring streets between the unruly and often aggressively hostile students and every level of authority—teachers, monitors, principal, security guard, police—establish a dysfunctional environment for everybody concerned, particularly for teachers who want to teach and pupils who want to learn.

These explosive conditions can be found in many inner-city junior and senior high schools; early warning signs are often found in the fifth- and sixth-grade classes. By the time a young person is two years behind in reading and has no special aptitude for arithmetic, school is likely to have little or no meaning. These students realize that they are not going far on the educational track; they find the classroom confining; they have no rapport with most or any of their teachers. Accordingly, a substantial minority—as many as a third or more—start to become truant; they join groups of older boys and girls who look for excitement on the city streets and often get into trouble with the law enforcement authorities.

The cycle of frustration in the educational system lasts for at least 10 years for many inner-city youngsters. Instead of acquiring the basic competencies that would help them to make the transition to the world of work, these youngsters have direct and powerful reinforcement of their belief that society has stacked the cards against them. They drop out or are pushed out of school and are not only short of skills but they are resistant to authority, unable to discipline themselves, and have few if any goals beyond having a good time.

Some analysts believe that the difficulties that many low-income, minority-group families experience in the inner-city are not much different from the difficulties experienced by most immigrant groups at the turn of this century. However, there are important distinctions between then and now. The first relates to differences in the community, the second to differences in the society. The history of Irish, Italian, and Jewish immigrant life in the large urban communities is replete with parallels of poverty, widespread crime, frequent family disruption, and conflict with older established groups on the periphery of the immigrant community. But the institutional sources of strength available to the earlier immigrants are lacking in most black and Hispanic ghettos. The most important mediating institution available earlier was active membership in the Catholic Church. Now that institution is much weaker or even absent. Additional support came from the ward politician, neighborhood organizations based on old world ties, and fraternal and trade union membership. While some of these supports exist in the contemporary inner-city, several have been weakened.

One of the disappointments in the arena of educational reform has been the limited success of community control of local schools. The members of locally elected school boards have often been unable to clarify their goals or to garner enough power and influence to implement them. It is often said that their failure reflects the strengths of the establishment: the city's board of education, the teachers union, local government. Whatever the explanation, the weakness of neighborhood leaders, the entrenched power of long-established groups, or both, the results have led to pitifully little reform.

There is another important societal difference between the earlier immigrants and the new minority groups. American society was never friendly to the immigrant, not even to those who spoke English. I recall a private meeting at which John Gardner asked me to mediate between James Conant and the black leadership in New York City who were unsettled by his *Slums and Suburbs*. At one point Conant, on the defensive, said that he remembered his grandmother telling him of her positive feelings for black people. To introduce some relief, I interposed the remark that her feeling for blacks had to be put into the context of her greater dislike for the recently arrived Irish.

Even in Boston, as Stephan Thernstrom's analysis makes clear, blacks rather than Irish, Jews, or Italians were the permanently excluded group. WASPs were concerned about the upward mobility of Catholics and Jews whose language, culture, and behavior patterns appeared to differ so greatly from their own. But these alien traits could be shed through education, money, and before the ecumenical era, by conversion. The only alien trait that is indelible is color. To see the fate and future of the black community, even at this late date, as parallel to that of the earlier immigrant groups is to ignore the pervasiveness of racism in American life. As I pointed out some years ago in *The Troublesome Presence: American Democracy and the Negro*, every President from George Washington to William Howard Taft saw no solution for the Negro other than emigration!

⚰ The core of racism is to send to all blacks from their earliest days the message that they belong to an inferior group apart from the rest of society, and that they can never join the body politic on a basis of full equality. The corrosion of mind and spirit resulting from racism is hard for a white person to imagine and even harder to acknowledge. An increasingly common response of whites is simply to deny the pervasiveness of racism or its inherent destructiveness.

✯ But blacks know better, and those who are fortunate enough to have escaped from the depressed circumstances of so many of their cohorts often continue in many different ways—through relocation, through new social contacts, through sending their children to predominantly white schools—to insure that they will not be pulled back into the quagmire of poverty and oppression. While the upwardly mobile of all races and classes have manifested similar fears and have engaged in similar behavior, we find relatively little family and community self-help in these early decades of black advance. Accordingly, the more disadvantaged who remain trapped in the most depressed areas of the inner-city receive less help and support from their successful relatives and neighbors than appears to have been the case with the earlier immigrants from Europe.

⚘The other critical difference between then and now, between the European immigrants and the Southern blacks who have relocated in the North and West (as well as those who have moved to the urban centers of the South), is the transformation of the U.S. economy and particularly the shifts in occupational structure. It was standard practice for many years in the New York harbor to have labor recruiters for large construction projects meet the boats arriving from Europe and ask the disembarking young men to roll up their sleeves so that they could look at their arm muscles. Those who passed were given a slip of paper that told them where to report on the following day to begin work. It made no difference if they could speak English; the job was theirs if they could put in a good day's physical work.

Today, however, the white-collar economy increasingly characterizes most of our largest cities, of which New York City is the epitome: only one out of every seven jobs is still in manufacturing or construction; the other six are in office or service work. This has significantly restricted employment opportunities to those who not only know English but are able to function in an environment increasingly dominated by words, numbers, and concepts. There are service jobs where literacy requirements are modest, even nonexistent, but most of them pay minimum wages and offer no long-term career opportunities.

To a much greater degree than in generations past, the competition for the good jobs with good incomes that permit one to lead a good life is largely determined by what transpires in school. Those who are good students, who learn to negotiate the educational system, and who can stay on the track until they acquire a professional degree have a significant advantage over those with lesser credentials. The converse is even more telling. Those who do not graduate enter the labor market handicapped. While a few will overcome their initial disabilities by a combination of skill acquisition, hard work, and luck, most will not.

Another observation focuses on teenage girls from low-income and minority-group families who are forced to drop out of high school because of pregnancy and the birth of a child. The numbers are horrendous—about a million pregnancies and over half a million live births to teenagers per year, most of whom are not married. Young blacks account for a disproportionate percentage of teenage mothers.

The cumulative deficits that follow from a young woman's interruption of her schooling to rear her offspring are great indeed. Even if she becomes, as most do, eligible for welfare, she will find it difficult, if not impossible, to return to school or to acquire a skill and a job that will yield sufficient income to free her from continued dependency on the Welfare Department. If she should have a second child out of wedlock, her fate becomes even bleaker.

Since information about and access to contraception is readily available, and since abortions during the first trimester are now legal (but no longer broadly available to those dependent on Medicaid), we must look further for an explanation of why so many teenagers, particularly black women, have children out of wedlock. Although the black community has generally not been as disapproving of out-of-wedlock children as the white community, this tolerance cannot cancel out the substantial difficulties that confront a young black mother who is forced to stop her schooling prior to graduation to care for herself and her child.

In this chapter I have sought to indicate the manner in which deficits in development accumulate in the lives of young people who are born into families handicapped by the absence of a father, low income, racial discrimination, and living in a deteriorating neighborhood.

I believe that it is a mistake to analyze the problems of young people primarily in terms of differential family income. In the first place, we have no way of relating developmental difficulties to differences in family income, particularly when we account for the substantial differences in regional standards of living and the non-cash income available to these families from public sources. Only gross differentials are likely to be meaningful—those resulting in inadequate nutrition, neglect of basic medical problems, the absence of any "disposable income" beyond expenditures for essentials. But although narrow differentials in income are not significant, race, residential location (access to public services), and welfare status are likely to have serious effects on the employability of young people.

Beyond these realities lies the critically important family emotional support system and, in the case of so many poor children, the relations between the mother and the children. While income and other economic realities affect this system, they do not determine it; and this goes far to explain why some children in deprived circumstances make it and others do not. The relations between mother and child are critical for the latter's development.

This last factor has bearing throughout the entire income distribution of families, not only for those at the bottom of the income scale but for those through the middle range all the way to the top. There is otherwise no explanation of why so many young people from middle- and upper-income families undergo a disturbed developmental process that frequently is masked until late adolescence or young adulthood. It then leads them into drug use and other aberrant behavior. Often

31

they are unable to hold a job. The advantage of family resources is that many of the less disturbed among these young people will, after some years of turmoil, be able to pull themselves together, although some fail despite having considerable family support.

In reviewing the roles of the principal shaping institutions—family, school, community, and society—we have found that the developmental stages through which young people pass are conditioned by the ability of these institutions to perform their essential functions. If they fail in whole or in part, the young person will be handicapped in coping with opportunities that are presented. Societal interventions, as we shall see, have been unable to compensate for serious shortfalls in the performance of the two principal developmental institutions, family and school.

Four:
The Military as a Developmental Experience

From 1940 until 1973 males in their late teens and in their twenties were subject to being drafted for military service. During World War II men were drafted through age 36. Except in 1948 and 1949, after the rapid demobilization that followed World War II and before the hope of a peaceful world was dashed by the outbreak of hostilities in Korea, all young American males had to register for the draft.

In 1970 President Richard Nixon appointed the Gates Commission to consider whether this established mechanism of obtaining manpower for the armed forces could be replaced by an All Volunteer Force (AVF) and, if so, what adjustments in pay and other perquisites would be required to implement the new approach. After a thorough analysis, the Gates Commission concluded that the AVF was feasible and recommended its early establishment. It further recommended a substantial increase in the pay of first-term enlistees to match or even exceed the comparable wage in the civilian sector as the principal adjustment required to make AVF a reality. By 1973 the President and Congress had acted affirmatively, and the AVF replaced the draft. A year later, even registration with the Selective Service System was no longer required of young men upon reaching the age of 18.

In mid-1979, after 6 years of experience with the AVF, Congress had before it a series of proposals to modify the military manpower procurement system because of the following shortcomings: failure to meet the requirement of the annual accession of over 400,000 young men and women; the declining quality of the recruits defined in terms of educational achievement; racial imbalances (considerably more blacks than their proportion of the population); shortfalls in the reserve forces; increasing reliance of the armed forces on women and civilians; excessive costs; lack of equity; and lowered morale.

In addition to the above criticisms of the AVF, the hostage crisis in Iran and the Soviet military action in Afghanistan raised new concerns about military preparedness. In July 1980 the dormant Selective Service System was reactivated and all 19- and 20-year-old males were required to register. This action by Congress was taken to improve the mobilization potential of the nation by reducing the time required to call up additional recruits in times of national emergency. However, the draft was not reinstituted.

Paralleling this focus on minor or major reforms of the military manpower procurement system are new proposals for youth programs that are usually subsumed under the sobriquet of "national service." Since the 1960s several types of voluntary "national service" programs have been in operation at modest levels of enrollment. Examples are the Peace Corps, Vista, and Action, which provide assignments in the U.S. or abroad for young people who, for subsistence wages, undertake such social services as education, social organization and youth work. Most of those who volunteer and are accepted into these programs, particularly the Peace Corps and Vista, are college graduates from middle-income homes. Often the young person considers such service as a continuance of his or her education.

Since the mid-1960s the federal government has also made various short-term work experience, training, and basic skills programs available to young people who need to improve their employability. Recently, these governmental programs have been increasingly targeted on youth from low-income families.

The renewed interest in national service programs comes from a variety of advocates with differing interests and goals. Some look to the gains that will accrue from a work experience directed at the accomplishment of national objectives; others to the channeling of unemployed or underemployed youth into socially desirable work not presently being accomplished because of taxpayer resistance to adding to the public payroll. Still others look to the improved opportunities for socialization, training, and work that would become available to hard-to-employ youth from such a large-scale and integrated effort; others to the possibility of dovetailing a much expanded national service effort with a strengthened military manpower procurement effort, thereby assuring that the armed forces will obtain recruits in the numbers and the quality it needs.

In this chapter, I shall review the lessons from three decades of compulsory military service that bear on the developmental experiences of young people. At the outset, let me voice the opinion that the advocates of either voluntary or compulsory national service programs have failed to understand the taxpayers' resistance to the costs involved, the difficulties of providing meaningful experiences for large numbers of young people, the lack of interest in service programs by most young people, and the substantial dangers of young people wasting one or two critical years in programs that do not serve their needs.

Here are a few observations about compulsory military service in the U.S. during the three decades when it was the law of the land. A first important distinction is whether a man was called to active duty and served during a period when the country was engaged in active conflict, i.e., 1941-1945, 1950-1953, or 1966-1971, or if he served when our military posture was simply defensive. The threat of being wounded or losing one's life made military service quite different for those who served during active hostilities, although even then the majority of the servicemen did not engage in active combat.

Another distinction is the length of time a young person remained in uniform. Those who were inducted in 1940 and whose length of service was automatically extended by legislation in 1941 served an average of six years before they were demobilized. Many of them were assigned to combat zones for most of their service. In contrast, the two-year draftees at various times during these three decades, were often released before their term was up, after 18 or 19 months of service, because the armed forces were approaching or exceeding their congressionally approved personnel ceilings.

Some servicemen never left the continental U.S.; others saw a good part of the world. In World War II, certain combat units saw action in North Africa, in Sicily, and again on the European front.

There were other important differences among those who had longer terms of service. Some had an opportunity to attend service schools and acquired a specific skill; others were shipped at the completion of their basic training to a combat unit where all of their additional training took place as a member of a squadron, battalion, or division.

These are a few of the differences that young men encountered in their military experiences. Consequently, it is difficult to talk about military service as a developmental experience without specifying the experiences of different individuals.

I now will attempt to sort out, at least in preliminary fashion, some of the important positive and negative experiences that military service afforded to young men, especially those who served during the 1970s. Since the focus of this book is on employability and employment, we will pay particular attention to the experiences that are most closely related to this aspect of their lives.

Some young people, especially those who have spent their childhood and adolescence in a small community and who come to the end of their schooling with few prospects of earning a livelihood in their immediate environs, find enlistment in one of the armed forces attractive. It offers them a host of opportunities (companionship, income, travel, medical services), including the prospect of acquiring a skill.

The armed forces recruit a large number of people from the South, particularly in areas long characterized by a declining agriculture and a slowly expanding manufacturing base with restricted employment opportunities. Recruitment of Southerners is also enhanced by the fact that the military tradition has a greater hold in that part of the country. Few of the nineteenth century immigrants who left Europe because they opposed conscription into the army of their native country, an anti-military attitude they retained in their adopted country, settled in the South.

The extent of regional variability with respect to the "positive propensity" of young men to serve in the U.S. Army is suggested by the following data collected in the fall of 1978 by the Youth Attitude Tracking Study. Restricting our focus to respondents who indicated that they were "definitely" considering serving in the Army, the range of responses around the national norm of 11.8% was from a low of 3.8% for New York City to a high of 18.2% for Alabama, Mississippi, and Tennessee. This almost five-fold difference was the largest recorded. Northern California was the other region that fell below the national norm, with a positive response of only 7.1%

Some 14% of respondents nationally had a "definite" interest in serving in the U.S. Navy. Once again, New York City had the lowest response rate (4.4%) and Ohio had the second lowest (8.9%). In light of the Ohio rate, it is hard to understand the above-average rates for Missouri and Indiana. With the exception of the response in those two midwestern states, the other regional data do not support the contention that the Navy has been able to draw disproportionately from the Midwest.

The report of youth attitudes toward the armed forces goes on to differentiate the "positive propensity" from the "negative propensity" individual along the following lines: the person inclined toward military service is more likely to be young, nonwhite, unemployed, and looking for work. He has a less educated father, has lesser mental ability, and is more concerned about all of the job attributes.

Let us consider briefly the extent to which the enlistee is likely to achieve his work and career goals. Many who enlist do not serve their initial three-year term. In 1974 more than one in every three enlistees was prematurely separated; the largest losses occurred within the first six months, followed by substantial losses of men in their second year of service.

Those who have studied attrition in the Army are impressed by the fact that the loss rate has been twice as great for non-high school graduates as for those who have earned a diploma. Not surprisingly, the Army stresses completing high school in its recruitment efforts. But the matter is more complex. It is difficult to determine whether the institutional bias in favor of high school graduates, which is based on the belief that they are easier to train and that they cause fewer disciplinary problems, operates as a self-fulfilling prophecy. As soon as a non-diploma holder gets into any difficulty, he is encouraged to leave the service.

On the basis of my eight-year study of *The Ineffective Soldier: Lessons for Management and the Nation* (Columbia University Press, 1959, 3 volumes), there are striking parallels in the personnel stance of the military of the mid- and late-1970s and its earlier behavior, not only in World War II but also in Korea and Vietnam eras. The rationalizations from one period to the next differ, but the basic stance remains the same. The military does not want to accept "low quality" personnel, and if it is forced to because of public pressure or labor market conditions, it moves to separate them at the earliest possible time.

Clearly, the substantial numbers of young people who were drafted and then released early cannot look back on their periods of active duty as positive developmental experiences. Early release carries the stigma of failure even if it is associated with an honorable discharge. However, even discharge need not be viewed as entirely negative, since even people who serve for a short time and get the right discharge are entitled to veterans' benefits of considerable value. The negative side of early separation is that many young people receive signals to the effect that society rewards them even though they failed to perform effectively.

The Military as a Developmental Experience

What can we learn about the career development of those who completed their first enlistment, usually three years? There is some sparse research that addressed the question of whether the experience of young men who served in the military in the post-World War II era had demonstrably positive outcomes in terms of their occupational and income gains. The findings from these "human capital" inquiries present no clear-cut demonstration of positive outcomes. But as we have seen, military service is a highly differentiated experience: one man learns to fly and another to walk with a heavy pack. Equally important is the fact that there were no effective controls in these studies. We know that throughout most of the post-World War II period, a high proportion of the better educated and more favored groups avoided induction into the service, and this complicates any attempt to assess the results of military service for those who enlisted or were drafted. Still we must try to piece together what we can about the following facets: socialization, education, skill training, career options, and goals.

Let us consider the socialization process that takes place within the military. Many young persons who enlist have never been away from the community into which they were born and where they have lived until their late teens. They have a restricted view of their state and region and know nothing of the nation and the world. Once in uniform they come into close and continuing contact with peers and adults who speak, think, act, and react differently from the people they have previously known. The young man in the next bunk may be of Chinese extraction and the barracks sergeant may be a black—a new and strange world for the white farm boy from the mountains of Tennessee or the Hispanic from El Paso.

Some of the "socialization" process seems far-fetched. I recall that during World War II, I picked up a much decorated sergeant and gave him a lift from Washington, D.C., to Fort Meade, Maryland. I asked him what his assignment was, now that he had been rotated from the front. He said he was busy teaching young recruits from the Tennessee hills to use soap and running water to wash themselves!

While it would be difficult to prove, it is reasonable to assume that living in close quarters with peers who belong to a group that one has considered as inferior since childhood will result in a lessening of prejudice. On the other hand, when blacks and whites compete for control over the illicit drug trade or the use of recreational facilities, tensions can be exacerbated. But I submit that on balance the conflicts are less frequent than the occasions of shared positive experiences.

The military is an organization based on discipline, and it provides an environment that many young men find supportive. They are under close and continuing supervision. They are told what to do, the amount of time they have to accomplish each task, the standards they must meet. For many who have never lived in a structured and supervised environment, this exposure to discipline, even including its occasional erratic and irrational demands, is a positive experience.

The military is a complex organization, and although most enlistees come into direct contact with only limited sectors and have no opportunity to see it as a whole, they do understand how the many parts are interrelated. In light of the dominance of large bureaucratic organizations in both the private sector (corporations and trade unions) and in the public sector (universities, hospitals, governmental agencies), three years of experience in the military is often good training for dealing with other large organizations. The important lesson that a few learn is that even a lowly private is not completely at the mercy of the bureaucracy. There are many ways to maneuver in order to obtain a better assignment.

While there was some decline in the quality of leadership at both the non-commissioned and commissioned officer level during the Vietnam War, many young men then and now have been exposed to leaders who by example, instruction, and counsel have been able to help enlistees clarify their goals and have better control over their lives.

The socialization process within the armed forces has additional dimensions including training in cleanliness, dress, health habits, diet, exercise, and exposure to recreational and cultural activities. The young enlistees must also learn to cope with separation from relatives and friends, and they face decisions about what to do with their money and their free time. All of these aspects of military life represent challenges. While some fail, most enlistees learn to cope with these challenges, and they leave the service with considerably more strength and sophistication than they had when they entered. Some may have learned the wrong things—how to avoid work, how to gamble, how to make money through illegal activities— but most leave with useful new knowledge and skills.

In 1966, under pressure from President Lyndon Johnson and the accelerating manpower needs to cope with the expansion of hostilities in Vietnam, the U.S. Department of

Defense instituted "Project One Hundred Thousand." Through that project the DoD adjusted its standards and agreed to accept enlistees and draftees who had previously been excluded because they fell below the cutoff point on the Armed Forces Qualification Test or because they failed to meet the physical requirements, even though their defects could be remedied through simple surgical or other medical interventions.

The three-year follow-up study released in December 1969 revealed that the overall performance record of those "new standards men" was remarkably similar to that of the control group in all respects—retention, training, occupational assignment, grade, disciplinary infractions—although on almost every count the control group was a few percentage points higher. A total of 246,000 persons were accepted under this special program, amounting to 11% of the new recruits. Among the important differences between the new standards men and the control group were:

Race: 40% were nonwhite compared to 9% of the controls

Education: 45% were high school graduates compared to 76% of the controls

Reading Ability: The median reading level was 6.3 compared to 10.9 for the controls

Region: Almost half were from the South compared to 28% of the controls.

In sum, the DoD accepted a greater number of Southern blacks with lower educational achievement than had been its practice in previous years. With respect to performance, almost all of the new standards men passed basic training (95%); 90% received initial skill training; 90% were rated by their supervisors as excellent or good; 50% were promoted to corporal or sergeant within their first term of service.

One of the interesting and constructive efforts in which the Army took the lead was to offer remedial reading programs to 10,000 men a year. Over 80% of the enrollees completed the program and gained between 1.8 and two years in reading ability, which brought their average reading ability to the sixth-grade level.

For a long time the armed forces have encouraged their enlisted personnel who do not have high school diplomas to pursue additional study in order to acquire a General Education Development (GED) certificate, which is broadly accepted by civilian employers as the equivalent of a high school diploma. A considerable number of the new standards men worked toward acquiring the GED.

On the basis of these selective findings from the three-year study, it is difficult to conclude that the experiment was anything but a success for the men, the military, and the nation. But the military leadership did not agree. As soon as the reduction in military personnel followed the termination of hostilities in Vietnam and the subsequent transition to the All Volunteer Force, enlistment standards were raised to a new high.

In addition to reading and other educational remedial work to which only relatively small numbers are exposed, the Army offers all enlisted men opportunities to participate in a wide variety of educational programs including current events, U.S. history, orientation to the foreign country to which they are assigned, sex education, and other subjects. While it would be difficult to reach an objective assessment of the value of these educational experiences to the employability of the young men exposed to them, they probably add to the enlistees' general knowledge, which may have a career benefit.

The more directly relevant experiences related to employability are the occupational training in military schools and on assignments. In 1978 the occupational distribution of active duty, enlisted, male personnel were distributed among the following principal areas:

**Enlisted Personnel, U.S. Department
of Defense, 1978**

Military and naval specialists	260,000
Electronic equipment repairmen	165,400
Communications and intelligence specialists	150,000
Medical and dental specialists	79,800
Other technical and allied specialists	37,200
Support and administration	266,500
Electrical/mechanical equipment repairmen	356,000
Craftsmen	70,700
Service and supply handlers	160,800
Non-occupational (patients, prisoners, students, and unclassified)	227,100

Of the approximately 1,700,000 enlisted personnel with an occupational specialty, approximately half are in a field of work that is closely related to the civilian economy. Only about one-third pursue duties, as military specialists or in functional support activities, that have little if any transferability.

Several observations are pertinent. First, a significant number of all enlistees—those who are assigned to combat units as well as the many who serve in supply and clerical positions—are likely to leave the service with few job-specific skills that will help them in their search for civilian employment. On the other hand, those who have acquired a level of skill in electronics, equipment repair, and other technical areas will be in a better position. In sum, the military does not provide every enlistee with a skill that is in demand in the civilian economy, but a significant number of all who spend three years on active duty do acquire a useful skill.

Most servicemen with an acceptable record have the opportunity to reenlist, and a steadily increasing percentage of first-timers are doing so. In 1977 more than 41% of DoD personnel had over four years of service compared to only 27% in the late 1960s. At a minimum, then, the career prospects of those who opt to remain on active duty and are permitted to reenlist have been improved. Those who want to leave the service or are forced out at the end of their first term are in better positions to find jobs because many employers place considerable weight on the applicant's having completed his tour of duty and having received an honorable discharge.

In other ways military service has helped to advance the career development of servicemen who return to civilian life. Until legislation that eliminated educational benefits to veterans went into effect in December 1977, a significant number of the new veterans took advantage of the opportunity to have some part of the costs of their further education or occupational training paid for by the Veterans Administration. In addition, the opportunities that many had while in the service to spend time in different locations within the United States as well as in some foreign countries broadened their knowledge of various labor markets and alternative living and working environments.

Enlistment in the All Volunteer Armed Forces also represents a career opportunity for blacks. In 1977 total black officer strength in the DoD numbered around 11,000, more than double the number in 1964. The number of blacks increased from under 2% to approximately 4% of total officer strength during this period. Most revealing is the fact that from 1972 to 1977 the percentage of black officers increased from 1.6% to 5.4%. This latter figure is close to the percentage of black males among all male college seniors, the principal pool from which the military recruits officer candidates.

The gains by blacks among enlisted men are even more substantial. About 9% of all youth who qualify for service under present standards are black, and from 1964 to 1977 the number of enlisted blacks increased from just under 10% to over 18%. In the Army, blacks account for about 30% of all new enlistees.

As we have seen, much of the opposition to the All Volunteer Armed Forces stems from the concern that a disproportionate number of blacks have entered the military, a concern that for some reflects a belief that no group should bear a disproportionate share of the risk in defending the nation and, for others, a fear of the potential power that blacks might gain from their disproportionate numbers in the military. But these policy considerations aside, there is no way to see these large gains for blacks except as a career opportunity for many who would otherwise have been unemployed or forced to settle for marginal jobs.

Equally revealing are the figures with respect to women. A recent DoD report said, "Women represent a major underutilized manpower resource." As recently as 1968, enlisted women on active duty accounted for less than 1% of all enlisted personnel. By 1979 the percentage stood at 7.5, and it is expected to grow to 11.6% by 1984.

These striking gains in participation in the military by women is only one part of the story. The other part relates to the revolution that has taken place in opening up assignments to women. Current Army policy states, "Women are authorized to serve in any officer or enlisted specialty except some selected specialties . . . [such as] infantry, armor, cannon field artillery, combat engineer . . . ."

Within the relatively few years since the effort to enlist more women and to broaden their assignments has been under way, women have been assigned to electronics equipment repair, communications, intelligence, electrical and medical equipment repair, craft trades, and technical work (other than medical and dental where they are overrepresented). With regard to retention, their rates parallel those of men except in the nontraditional fields, where they have only recently been accepted for training.

Since such a high percentage of young men have served in the military since 1940, it is disappointing that we know relatively little about the impact of their active duty on their occupational and career development. But the data and analysis presented in this chapter suggest that a tour of active

43

duty had a positive impact on the careers of a high, if unknown, proportion of all who served and particularly those who had the opportunity to acquire a skill that was transferable to the civilian economy. Even those who spent most or all of their time in a combat unit may have left the service with career benefits involving organizational know-how, labor market information, and veterans' benefits.

No national youth policy can ignore the impact of military service, not only because the armed forces must continue to recruit many of the eligible age group, but because of the impact of different patterns of military training and education on the young men and women who are recruited.

Five:
The Opportunity Matrix

S chooling is the intermediate stage in the developmental process; it falls between the early indoctrination and conditioning that occur within the family and the exposures and experiences that help to shape the young adult entering the world of work. Formal education involves a dynamic relationship between the individual seeking the service and the provider (both the institution and the staff). This relationship is special for young children since their behavior is subject to adult control. They are not asked whether they want to go to school. They must go. At the same time, they cannot be forced to listen to the teacher; the teacher can merely insist that the child does not disrupt the class.

The values and attitudes that young adults hold about the future affect their current behavior, and simultaneously current experiences help to shape their expectations of the future. Some analysts neglect this cycle of cause and effect, while other theorists have sought to explain too much about the differential behavior of various groups on the basis of such a cycle. The outstanding example of the latter are those theorists identified with the "culture of poverty" school that holds that many of the poor remain poor because, lacking inclination to postpone pleasure and to make a present investment to gain advantages in the future, they live only for the moment. But the history of this country is replete with illustrations that refute this viewpoint. Every immigrant group that arrived on these shores, sooner or later, extricated itself from the "culture of poverty." Edward Banfield, a proponent of the inability-to-postpone doctrine, has sought to differentiate the black masses in the urban ghettos from the earlier streams of immigrants, arguing that blacks are more present-oriented than the earlier immigrants. But this proposition is hard to maintain in the face of such varied evidence as the school enrollment data and gains in occupational status and income of the children of many inner-city blacks in recent decades.

Even if gross differences in the future-oriented behavior of whites and non-whites do not hold up, differences in how children from various racial and social class groups respond to school are worth exploring, particularly their perceptions of the job and career opportunities open to them and the extent to which schooling is relevant to their future.

To take the easier case first, consider the way in which most middle-class families influence the educational goals and schooling behavior of their offspring. I do not know of any research that speaks specifically to the question of how a young child in the home of a professional—physician, lawyer, teacher, engineer—perceives that he or she will stay in school for many years. The child of 6 or 8 has difficulty in comprehending "the future," particularly in relating his behavior to far off events. But each year increasing intellectual and emotional maturation makes it easier for the young person to understand what is expected in terms of future schooling and the gains that he or she can anticipate from it.

Youngsters between 8 and 11 have no clear-cut perception of the occupational hierarchy and the ways in which different jobs are linked through the educational system to earnings and career opportunities. But the young child does have some loose perceptions about the relative social and economic status of taxi drivers, shopkeepers, auto mechanics, lawyers, physicians, movie stars, and leading sports figures.

All of the family and emotional influences to which the middle-class youngster in a professional household is exposed reinforce each other to help him or her learn that a college degree is the pathway to a satisfactory adult role. Parents are likely to be interested in their child's experiences in school and create many opportunities outside and within the home to broaden educational experiences. Unless parents push too hard (and some do) or their youngster is emotionally or intellectually unable to keep up with his classmates, the typical child of professional parents takes the 16-year school cycle in stride. At the end of this period, some are already in a good position to pursue a career by having attended a prestigious university. Others may attempt to find an attractive job with no further education. Some will fail, but the vast majority, on the basis of their education and family connections, will get onto the lowest rung of the executive ladder and begin their upward climb.

The situation is vastly different for many young people from low-income homes, especially those brought up in a ghetto area where the schools are often physically run-down, the administration and teaching staff are beleaguered, and the environment both inside the school and in the neighborhood is dysfunctional for learning.

Shortly after the riots in the Watts district of Los Angeles in 1965, I spent some days in the community trying to understand what had happened and why in my capacity as chairman of the National Manpower Advisory Committee. Among the points that came to my attention was the fact that among the male high school dropouts were some of the brightest as well as some of the most backward students. Informed adults suggested that the alert, savvy youngsters had begun to realize that they were learning next to nothing in school; the teachers had given up making a serious effort to instruct them; school was more a detention pen than an educational institution. These youngsters had deduced from this that they would be better off on the streets where more interesting things were going on and where they would be free from oppressive constraints.

At about the same time several members of my staff and I were invited to meet with the counselors in some of the junior and senior high schools in Queens, New York City. We met in the library of a high school where the student body was nearly 100% black. Near the end of the morning session, one of my colleagues, noting that several students had been listening for a considerable time just outside the library, went over to inquire why they were there and was offered the following explanation: they had learned about the meeting and had decided that since nothing worthwhile was happening in their classes they might be able to pick up some useful ideas from our discussions. During the lunch break, I read the assignments in modern history on the bulletin board. These minority group students were required to memorize the names and dates of the rulers of France between Napoleon I and Napoleon III, a set of facts not likely to have much relevance to them.

Nigerian-born anthropologist John V. Ogbu, currently at the University of California-Berkeley, sought in *Minority Education and Caste: The American System in Cross Cultural Perspective* to explain the educational retardation of so large a proportion of black children. He did not focus on family poverty or on the inadequacies of the schools they attend but on the direct and indirect impact of their caste subordination, which has kept most blacks out of the mainstream of professional jobs and careers in America. Ogbu argues that from earliest childhood the black child understands that no matter what he does, how hard he tries, or how much he accomplishes, society is structured to cheat him of most of his just rewards. Under these conditions of exploitation, why should the black child make an effort to conform to the demands of white society, to subject himself to the discipline of his school, or to stop playing and do his homework? In the end these sacrifices will be to little or no avail, since his blackness will prevent him from enjoying the fruits of his efforts. From his earliest days of consciousness he hears his family, friends, and neighbors refer to the inequities and injustices that this caste society inflicts on blacks.

In 1952 The Rockefeller Brothers Fund made a grant to the National Urban League to enable its trustees to reappraise their program. I was asked to present one of the papers which I titled "Better Preparation for Better Jobs." I argued that job opportunities were at long last opening up for the black minority at a rate faster than they were being educated to fill them, especially in the professional, managerial, and technical fields.

This discrepancy between educational preparation and expanded job opportunities is easy to understand when one recalls the pervasive and deep-seated discrimination against blacks that had placed almost insuperable barriers in their path for several generations after the Civil War. A deeply segregated society continued to subordinate the black population, particularly to assure that the white majority would not have to contend with the competition of blacks for the better jobs that are always in relatively scarce supply.

The labor market had become a little less discriminatory during World War II and the Korean War. Demographers were suggesting that if the economy continued its generally upbeat trend and if racial antagonism diminished, more desirable job and career opportunities would be available to qualified black men and women. For this reason I emphasized that increasing numbers of minority group members had to complete higher education.

The *Brown* decision in 1954, the passage in 1958 of the first federal Civil Rights Act since Reconstruction, and the substantial drop in discriminatory attitudes and behavior among large sectors of the American public all contributed to creating a more favorable environment for blacks to remain in school and to acquire a high school diploma or college degree. Many blacks responded; however, the cumulative deficits of the past were not easily neutralized.

Many black youngsters and their parents did not believe that the signs pointing to a lowering of the employment barriers were real. There was a suspicion that even if the young black person made a special effort to get an education and did well in his or her studies, a desirable job opportunity

48

would not be available at the end of the road. It was asking a lot of a black American to have faith in the promises of sympathetic whites, who had been unable to deliver in the past. A quarter of a century later, in the late 1970s, similar tensions continued to exist among many from black, low-income homes, despite a growing awareness that a significant increase has taken place in the number of blacks moving into better jobs and up the career ladders.

In the most deprived sections of the urban ghettos, young children see pimps, hustlers, and gamblers as the big spenders, the best dressed, and with the biggest cars—in short, the successful ones. They do not need to be told that these individuals have become successful without the benefits of extended schooling, surely without having demonstrated outstanding academic achievement. Many children in the elementary grades know no one for whom school has been the key to a better job and a better life. Their parents may stress that a good education will pay off, but for many this claim is not anchored in their own experience. They must accept it on faith.

Those who find the classroom reasonably interesting, if not exciting, may decide to conform, to listen, to follow orders, to do their homework, to put forth their best efforts. But many others quite early in their schooling look upon the school as an alien, if not hostile, environment that has little to offer them.

The young are particularly sensitive to whether or not adults like them. And many teachers, in seeking to control the class, resort to punishing the innocent along with the guilty for infractions of discipline. To these youngsters the world inside the school quickly resembles the world outside. It is full of hostile people who have no interest in or sympathy for them. Fortunately, in the earliest grades, only a minority of youngsters seriously offend their teachers. Even an immature teacher with little or no experience in a ghetto school can control a class of six- or seven-year-olds, although he or she may have less success in teaching them to read and do arithmetic.

By the fifth or sixth grade, the classroom in the typical ghetto school is likely to become dysfunctional for learning. The older children in the class generally are those who have failed to master the minimum skills required to be promoted to the next grade. Older and bigger than their classmates and finding the classroom boring and oppressive, they seek diversion and start annoying students who sit next to them, precipitating arguments with the teacher, and otherwise engag-

49

ing in disruptive tactics. Their goals and those of the teacher are diametrically opposed: they want trouble, or at least excitement; the teacher needs quiet to carry out the lesson. Many students get caught in the middle, preferring to learn but also wanting to identify with the disruptive leaders who often claim that they are "sticking up" for their classmates whom the "system" mistreats.

In the face of so much disturbance, many teachers give up trying to instruct, and their attitudes lead to the estrangement of those students who were not initially disruptive. The continuing battle that usually intensifies in the upper grades includes not only the students and the classroom teachers but also the administration, the food service attendants, the security guards, and everybody else in a position of power. In light of so much turmoil and confusion, the one- or two-year retardation in reading or arithmetic that is characteristic of so many students in ghetto schools is not surprising. Nevertheless, many students profit from their educational experience despite the many negatives in their environment.

A particularly negative experience that has confronted many youngsters from minority groups over the years is the subtle urging they receive from their teachers and counselors to prepare for the manual trades or services and not to pursue academic subjects that would lead to college and a professional career. Their advisors reinforce these recommendations with an analysis of the occupational distribution of blacks in the nation and in the community that proves that most blacks are employed in manual and service occupations and that only a handful have penetrated the professions and white collar work.

But these advisors are deaf and blind to the long-suppressed aspirations of generations of blacks. Now that the discriminatory barriers have finally been lowered, many as a direct consequence of blacks taking to the streets to force the issue, young blacks today are determined to obtain access to the better jobs. Many counselors fail to recognize that the under-representation of blacks in white collar employment is paralleled by their substantial exclusion from better paying jobs in the construction trades, transportation, and public utilities. It was not until the late 1960s that significant progress was made to open apprenticeships to blacks and other minorities. The career guidance that black youngsters received prior to that time, which directed them to blue collar or service jobs, was directed to preparing them for the least skilled, lowest paying jobs in the American economy.

50

Many middle- and upper-class whites, particularly those in the South, were distressed that they could no longer find a black woman who was willing to do housework, cooking, and child rearing for a few dollars a week, two meals a day, and the right to "tote" some food. Roosevelt's New Deal had undermined the old structure by providing alternatives in the form of the Works Progress Administration (WPA) and Aid to Dependent Children. The expanding economy of the Fifties and Sixties opened a range of factory and office jobs to black women in both the South and the North, which helped to dry up the pool of domestic servants.

Many white women who wanted household help insisted that they were willing to pay good wages and offer good working conditions, but they were unable to find "reliable" help. Their complaints were both true and false. It was true that the salaries offered were often competitive with the lower wages in the rest of the economy, and domestic workers frequently had additional benefits such as meals and a room. But the hours of work were longer, the days off fewer, fringe benefits such as health and pension benefits were nonexistent, the terms of employment were more personal, and there were no restraints on the employer's freedom to discharge.

Regardless of these objective considerations, young black women had not waited for their long-delayed emancipation to do voluntarily what their mothers and grandmothers had earlier done under economic and social duress, that is, to be a servant to white people under the direct and often oppressive supervision of the woman of the house. It is not surprising, therefore, that there has been a steady decline in the number of black women in domestic service—from 1,932,000 in 1958 to 1,135,000 in 1978.

Another facet of the relationship of education to jobs has attracted considerable attention during recent decades from both our political leaders and our social scientists. In 1957 the launching of Sputnik convinced our political leaders that the future of the United States was in jeopardy, because we had failed to pay adequate attention to the full development of the nation's talent. Many young people who had achieved good academic records in high school did not enter or did not graduate from college because of the financial costs involved in remaining out of the labor market for four years while paying tuition and living expenses. While those at the very top of their class might obtain a partial or a full scholarship, many others who were close to the top could not afford to go to college.

In the following years, a great deal of federal and state money was appropriated to make scholarships, earning opportunities, and loans available so that almost all qualified students could continue with their studies. Finances would no longer be a barrier. To encourage vastly larger numbers to pursue higher education, our leaders, starting with President Eisenhower and continuing to President Ford, urged young people to get as much education as possible, on the ground that they would thereby assure themselves of a good job, a good career, a good life.

In 1964 Gary Becker published *Human Capital*, which articulated the relationships between educational achievement and lifetime earnings. His was an elaboration of Alfred Marshall's 1890 theory of investment in human beings that states that the amount of investment devoted to acquiring a skill was directly related to future earnings. The evidence was unequivocal: those who went to school for only eight years earned considerably less than those with a high school diploma. Similarly, those with a college or a higher degree earned considerably more than those who stopped at the end of high school. While the specialists disagreed on the fine points, such as the rate of discount to be applied over the working life of an individual and how to differentiate between native talent and years of schooling, they did agree that college graduates earned about $150,000 more than high school graduates over a lifetime. The educational leadership then undertook to indoctrinate the legislators in the new human capital approach in order to gain increased appropriations.

Some of the early skeptics, of which I was one, warned that the theory was defective in its treatment of women, whose education did not appear to be directly correlated with lifetime earnings. While the figures supported the theory that more education was a good investment, they were valid only in considering the averages; the dispersal around the averages was considerable since plumbers and other craftsmen with a high school education or less often earned considerably more than teachers, ministers, and librarians who had four or more years of additional education. Or, put slightly differently, between one-fifth and one-quarter of all college graduates were employed in jobs that were at the same income level as those held by high school graduates.

Eventually, the most vulnerable aspect of the new doctrine stemmed from its persuasiveness. If more and more young people heeded its message, the supply of college-trained persons would increase so that the earlier supply-demand relationships would no longer hold, and the greater numbers of college graduates would inevitably force the earnings of the educated to decline. In 1976 Richard Freeman of Harvard University published his interesting monograph, *The Overeducated American*, in which he analyzed the ways in which the market adjusted to the excessive number of college graduates.

Freeman was a relative latecomer into the field of those who raised questions about the value of more education for the purposes of occupational and income mobility. Some critics, remembering Blau and Duncan's carefully crafted study, *The American Occupational Structure*, called attention to the relatively slow changes in the occupational profiles of successive generations. The sons of farmers on the average did not move more than one or two steps up the hierarchy; most of them remained farmers, a few became craftsmen, and a very few moved into the better-paying white collar occupations. Even a rapidly expanding American economy did not permit the children of fathers in the lower half of the occupational hierarchy to catapult to the top rungs. Economic growth, differential birth rates, and native ability, afforded some room for movement in both directions; some in the higher levels slipped down, a larger number were able to advance. But again, the movements were usually only one or at the most two grades on a 10-grade scale.

In *Equality*, Christopher Jencks provided an extended review of the statistical data he was able to marshall about the relationships between education and equality. He concluded that access to schooling alone effected little change in the relative positions of large groups. To reduce the inequality that is prevalent in American society, Jencks stipulated, the country must undertake a frontal attack on income distribution; the pathway through the schools promised little.

Another critic of the hypothesis that salvation could be achieved through education is my colleague, Ivar Berg, who in *Education and Jobs*, called attention to confusion about education as skill, education as credentials, education as productivity, and education as earnings. Berg believes that it is erroneous to assume that because the better educated obtain the better jobs that they are more productive and entitled to higher earnings. Each of these relations can be questioned, and Berg presents evidence that throws doubt on the conventional wisdom.

⚹ What generalizations can be drawn from this review of the manner in which the family and the school interact to condition the opportunities of young people to obtain preferred jobs? To the extent that preferred jobs require a college degree and frequently more education, those who are born into families where an advanced education is taken for granted have the edge. This is true for a significant number of youngsters from middle-class families, particularly where one or both parents are college graduates.

At the opposite extreme are youngsters from low-income families in minority groups, most of whom live in run-down areas of the inner city, whose school experiences are negative because of the strangeness of language, lack of rapport between them and their teachers, a rigid discipline that is sharply confining, and limited understanding and involvement of their parents in what transpires in school.

These incipient tensions and conflicts are compounded in many ghetto schools where by the fifth and sixth grade, classes are dominated by noise and strife. Because the teacher must attempt to control the troublemakers, he or she has no time, energy, or inclination to teach the rest of the class. Here is the source of retardation in learning, truancy, and early dropouts. Despite the dysfunctional environment that characterizes many ghetto schools, a growing percentage of minority youth do make it through high school and significantly larger numbers enter and complete college. The gap between whites and blacks has narrowed appreciably, although it remains substantial.

⚹ Other factors in securing employment are also important; family, friends, location, and racial and sex discrimination are among the most significant. The labor market literature leaves no questions that most people get jobs through the intervention of relatives and friends. Those at the bottom of the hierarchy are least able to benefit from such a network. The heavy concentration of the black population in the older cities of the North at a time when manufacturing has moved out to the suburbs and recently to the expanding regions of the Sunbelt has introduced a particular handicap for black youths in finding jobs. This is particularly so for those who are ill-prepared for the white collar employment that dominates most urban markets.

⚹ Finally, discrimination continues to be a potent force in restricting the number and quality of positions available to black youth. Although some employers want to hire minorities

54

so that they will be in compliance with the federal Equal Employment Opportunity regulations, discrimination continues to exist and to be a real impediment in the search for decent jobs by black youngsters.

Belief in education as the solution to the problems of the nation and the individual, which became firmly entrenched in the 1950s and again in the 1960s, started at a time when the nation's economy was performing well. Through one or another circumstance, including the acquisition of an education, many young people and adults were able to improve their job prospects and move up the career ladder. Most of the offspring of middle-class white families did well, and many of the long-excluded black population improved their educational and employment opportunities as reflected in the sizable gains that young blacks have made in their occupational distribution, job and career prospects, and earnings. Unfortunately, the momentum of the Sixties was not maintained in the Seventies, and there was consequent deterioration in the prospects of those black youngsters who could not acquire high school diplomas. It is this population that reaches working age at a disadvantage in their attempts to make the transition to adulthood.

Six:
The Facilitators

L ong before the nation became aware of the high incidence
of unemployment among teenagers and young adults in
the late 1960s and early 1970s, our society had set up a variety
of mechanisms aimed at improving the developmental prospects for young people. Some were directed at facilitating the
transition from family to school, some to improving the
educational and career options for young people and assisting
them to acquire relevant skills, some to strengthening the
transitional process from school to work.

In this chapter I shall review selectively the more important of these facilitators and assess their potential and limitations for different groups of young people, particularly those
most in need of assistance.

The development of nursery schools and kindergartens
has enabled a growing number of 3-, 4-, and 5-year-olds to be
engaged, usually for half a day, in organized play that has
built-in learning components. Middle- and upper-income
parents have been attracted to these facilities, particularly
nursery schools, which, until the advent of Head Start in the
mid-1960s, were financed almost exclusively by private tuition.

Apart from learning considerations, participation in group
activities for children between the ages of 3 and 6 is likely to
ease the trauma of entering elementary school. By the time
the child has experienced separation from his or her mother,
has had to conform to group pressures, has had to accept the
teacher as a surrogate parent, he or she is better prepared to
cope with the discipline that comes with formal education in
the first grade.

I noted earlier that evaluations of the Head Start program
did not reveal a continued improvement in test scores after
these children started school. Apparently, whatever gains
they achieved from participating in Head Start in terms of
their ability to cope with the school curriculum were cancelled
out by the dysfunctional elements in their environment. In
light of the severe environmental deprivations of many Head
Start children, it is questionable whether any type of social
intervention will result in changing the outcomes for many of
the disadvantaged.

Since the mid-1960s the federal government has made annual grants to school districts to assist them in expanding

and improving the resources available to schools that enroll large numbers of children from low-income families.

As with so many grant-in-aid programs, the flow of federal funds initially did not reach more than a small number of the pupils for whom they were intended. Some Title I and Title II money was sometimes made available to school districts with only a few disadvantaged pupils. Additional mismanagement occurred in the allocations within schools that had children from middle-class homes as well as disadvantaged youngsters. For a considerable time there was little effective monitoring to insure that the funds were allocated to those most in need of assistance. In theory, the funds should have been spent largely to employ teaching assistants and specialists to work with students who could not keep pace with the rest of the class in reading, spelling, arithmetic, and other subjects.

The saddest finding was the discovery that, even where the funds went to help the pupils most in need of assistance by providing additional staff, the results were often equivocal. The gains in competence, at least according to the test instruments, were at best quite modest. This suggests that if the public school system cannot teach the 3 Rs to youngsters from low-income families, especially those from minority groups, it is unlikely that enrichment programs that use the same books and the same methods and that operate in the same constrained environment can alter the learning curve.

Reformulated, the proposition might state that if a major institution cannot perform its principal mission, manipulations at the margin are not likely to correct many of the weaknesses. I am reminded of what transpired at Imperial Chemical Industries in Britain at the beginning of World War II. The scientists and engineers were unhappy with their work environment and their incentives and rewards. The dissatisfaction finally came to the attention of the top management, who responded by giving these professionals access to the executive dining room! Even in a class-conscious society such as Great Britain, where the trappings of status are important, this "solution" fell on its face. The roots of the trouble were deeper and were not affected by the proposed accommodation.

Between 1966 and 1971 the New York City public schools added approximately 17,000 teacher aides and other paraprofessionals at an annual cost of over $22 million. During the same period the reading scores of the pupils in the elementary schools did not show any improvement; in fact, they declined. The specific intervention device, teacher aides, clearly was ineffective, at least in terms of reading improvement.

In the late Sixties and early Seventies, U.S. Commissioner of Education Sidney Marland, aware of the difficulties that many high school students were experiencing in making a satisfactory transition to the world of work, suggested a new type of intervention, one that he dubbed "career education." His basic assumption was that the schools were not giving adequate attention to preparing students for the world of work. He and his associates designed a series of specific programs, all aimed at bringing the school and work place into closer alignment. Marland believed that if young people, even in the early grades and surely by the end of elementary school, were taught about occupations and careers, they would be able to relate their school instruction to the opportunities they would confront later on in the educational system, in training institutions, and in the world of work.

At the thirty-second meeting of the National Manpower Advisory Committee in December 1971, Commissioner Marland set out the following five objectives for the school systems:

1. To help young people to avoid failure in school;
2. To help them to develop a sound self-identity;
3. To deflect large numbers of unqualified youngsters from the mirage of college;
4. To raise the status of jobs that did not require a college degree;
5. To enable people to move back and forth between school and work in accordance with their changing expectations and needs.

In my letter to the Secretary of Labor after this meeting, the following summary of this discussion appeared:

> Our committee, while strongly in sympathy with the Commissioner's new approach, raised the following caveats, more as constructive criticism than in opposition to "career education" as an idea, a plan, or a program:
> a.　Great care must be taken to avoid work/study programs as a back entrance into child labor.
> b.　Career education may be used to discourage the disadvantaged from seeking admission to college; this in turn might prevent some of them from rising on the social and economic ladder.
> c.　The educational planners must exercise caution not to "oversell" the new approach, which can work only to the extent that employment and career opportunities for all people are improved.

d. It will be necessary to elicit the support of the academically oriented educational community in this effort. If vocational educators take over, the effort is doomed because they alone cannot restructure the educational establishment.

e. The reform must be mounted with the realization that little if any new money will be made available by a resentful electorate which feels that it has been oversold on education.

f. The capability of the federal government to bring about the specific reforms required at local and state levels is limited; consequently, multiple models in the field which can serve as demonstration projects are desirable.

g. Guidance and counseling, which is conspicuously weak in the career arena, is critical.

h. It will be necessary to loosen the importance of credentialing; otherwise, career education cannot succeed.

i. The proponents of the new program must not oversell it. With limited opportunities and with the unemployment rates at an unacceptable level, many people will be unable to find suitable work regardless of how they are educated or trained.

j. It is impossible at present to develop sound manpower forecasts. Hence career education must present opportunities for retraining to help people refit themselves into a changing economy.

k. The school system must be reformed so that it can perform its basic task of providing basic knowledge and skills.

l. There is a danger that the federal government will once again perform good prelaunch efforts and fund a few interesting experimental and demonstration projects but will fail to mount the long-term efforts required for carrying through a major reform.

m. It will be necessary to test the assumption that business will cooperate in providing opportunities for good work/study programs.

n. It will be desirable to study the European experience in depth, since Germany, Sweden, the United Kingdom, and other countries have experimented selectively with career education.

o. Paper planning in Washington must not be confused with broad support in the hinterland. At present, national interest and support for career education is modest. More dialogue and involvement are required.

p. Education must be considered a consumption as well as an investment goal. The work force is already conspicuously overtrained for the jobs available, and widespread discontent has resulted.

With the advantage of hindsight it is hard to find fault with any of the foregoing caveats. It is my view that career education, in promise and even more in reality, never came close to addressing the lack of effective articulation between school and work.

Nowhere can this be better seen than in the weakness of the guidance function in the school system. Starting in Boston in the first decade of this century as a service to assist young people who had to find work, school guidance went through a tortuous evolution; it got lost in testing in the 1920s and in developmental psychology in the 1930s, after which almost all aspects of career guidance disappeared (see my *Career Guidance: Who Needs It, Who Provides It, Who Can Improve It*, McGraw-Hill, 1971).

While there has been some refocusing on jobs and careers in recent years, school guidance counselors in high schools, where a high percentage of the student body goes on to college, spend most of their time in college placement. In the large city schools, much of the time and effort of counselors have been preempted with disciplinary problems, a role that makes their advisory function even more equivocal in the eyes of most students. Many counselors in ghetto schools are handicapped by their limited knowledge of the realities of the labor market, and they are also ineffective in helping their students to learn about and to apply to desirable training programs for jobs with a future. To compound matters even further, many counselors believed they were being helpful when they steered blacks and Hispanics away from college, away from jobs and careers that they, the counselors, thought were unrealistic in terms of the limited opportunities available in the discriminatory world. Some gave poor advice out of ignorance, others out of prejudice, but probably as many minority students were poorly counseled as profited from the advice they received.

Our society now relies on experts and specialists to compensate for the adverse environmental circumstances that afflict so many. This highly selective review of career guidance in the schools, which is now entering its seventh decade, is a warning that reliance on specialists is no guarantee that social outcomes will be improved. Iatrogenic results are not limited to medicine!

Let us now consider briefly the development of occupational and vocational courses, work-study programs, community colleges, and other post-secondary education programs as they relate to manpower training and the labor market.

Vocational and technical training in high school began in the late nineteenth century, but these programs began to grow with the increase in young people who stayed in school beyond the first eight grades. At that time many educators concluded that the traditional academic curriculum was not responsive to the needs of these young people, most of whom would remain in high school for little more than a year or two, after which they would have to find jobs. Seeking an alternative, educators began to emphasize skill training as a means of providing a transition into the world of work. Such efforts were supported by employers who saw the advantages to their future workers of having some knowledge about tools, shop arithmetic, and working with wood and metals.

Despite its earlier stance against becoming directly involved in any type of support for public education, the federal government decided during World War I that it should help expand vocational education in the interests of national defense, and it has continued its participation as a junior partner from that day to this. But most of the financial support for vocational education comes from state and local governments with occasional contributions from local employers.

As with most evaluations of social and particularly educational programs, there is considerable disagreement about whether vocational education has been a worthwhile investment for society and the individual. Its protagonists point to the competition for admission to vocational schools and to the job placement and earnings records of their graduates. The skeptics express concern about the substantially higher costs, the difficulties of maintaining up-to-date equipment and competent staff, the large numbers of students who encounter difficulties finding jobs because they have been trained in skills not needed in the labor market, employers' preference to do their own training, and the "creaming" that deflects students who should be encouraged to pursue a college-preparatory course. Among the other negatives that concern the skeptics is the finding of my colleague, Beatrice Reubens, that the differential employment and earnings experience of vocational versus other students does not hold over any length of time.

My own views are influenced by the following considerations: A serious vocational program requires that students be able to read instructions, do shop math, and follow blueprints. Even if the critical issues of cost, equipment, and staffing could be handled, there is still a poor match between most vocational programs and those students who at 14 or 15 are unable to do their regular school work. Vocational education, as presently structured and operating, is not responsive to the majority of the hard-to-educate students. An outsider sees vocational education at the secondary school level as difficult to structure, difficult to staff and finance, and unresponsive to students who do not have basic competencies.

This judgment, however, does not preclude a potential role for a vocational component in the curriculum for the nonacademic student. There is no other alternative. Regrettably, the leaders of vocational education have not been interested in this difficult but important task of experimenting with ways of using vocational elements to catch the interest and facilitate the basic learning of numbers, reading, and abstract thinking—all competencies that the educational system should provide to all students.

Let us consider those young people who, because they drop out early, are likely to encounter the most difficulties in finding and holding jobs. One model of vocational education in many secondary schools goes under the name of work-study or cooperative education. The typical arrangements provide for students to divide the day between school and work, or to follow a schedule of one week in school and the next in the work force. Such programs have the potential of giving direct meaning to what goes on in school. Unfortunately, only a small percent of those students who might profit from such programs can be placed.

The motivation of employers who enter into cooperative programs with the schools are sometimes altruistic, but they can also use these programs to recruit good workers. Accordingly, employers such as department stores, the telephone company, or an expanding manufacturing company, able to absorb a number of 17- or 18-year-olds into their regular work force, may benefit by hiring young people and helping them to adapt to the work place while they are still on the school rolls. But these employers do not want to hire the hard-to-teach, who are also likely to be the hard-to-employ. Rather, if they enter into a work-study plan they will look to the school to select those who are most likely to make the transition to the workplace with the least difficulty.

As with the selectivity of students for full-time vocational educational programs, so in the case of work-study programs, the group that most needs exposure to work, to adults, and to earning money are largely excluded. Quality vocational programs, in and out of school, are highly selective.

During the last two decades there has been a proliferation of area technical institutions that serve a larger geographic area and that provide a wider range of occupational skills with better equipment and skilled staff. There has also been marked expansion of junior and community colleges that usually offer three parallel tracks—academic, occupational, and cultural and leisure-time courses. Admission requirements differ among these institutions depending on whether the student is taking an occasional course or is working toward a degree. For the most part they do not accept high school dropouts, a group that might profit from the opportunity to re-enter the educational system after some years of knocking around the labor market. On the other hand, these institutions with their heavy occupational thrust have provided a wide range of opportunities for high school graduates who seek to enter the labor market after having acquired technical training, particularly in such fields as electronics, computers, health services, drafting, and other fields that provide access to the burgeoning service occupations.

The general impression of informed observers is that community colleges have prospered in no small measure because their programs are more flexible than high school-based vocational programs. Community college leaders have sought to work more closely with local employers and respond as quickly as possible to their shifting needs.

Many who attend community colleges do so after working hours and on weekends, further evidence of the flexibility of the new structures. Many students who hold full- or part-time positions can take courses to advance in the field in which they are employed, while others seek new skills to improve their employment and career prospects.

Finances must also be considered in this selective review of major trends in the recent past that have affected the occupational preparation of young people as they move through the educational system. There has long been considerable governmental (primarily state) and philanthropic funding for higher education in the United States. State participation on a sizable scale dates from the first half of the nineteenth century. The federal government became an important participant via the liberal GI benefits made available to veterans at the end of World War II and continuing until the end of 1977. A great many young people re-entered the educational-training system after their military service on the basis of these benefits; without them, these young people would have been forced to find jobs as quickly as possible.

The second major contribution of the federal government was the new funding it made available after Sputnik via the National Defense Education Act, which provided scholarships and fellowships for many students who were willing to pursue a course of study in science, engineering, foreign languages, or other disciplines Congress had designated as being directly connected to strengthening our national defense.

In the 1960s and 1970s Congress enacted and amended a series of acts that made grants and loans available to a significant number of college and graduate students. Between 1970 and 1978 federal grants (not loans) for higher education—research, facilities, and student assistance—increased from just under $4 billion to just over $8 billion, with the largest amount concentrated on student assistance. The Basic Educational Opportunity Grant Program initiated by the federal government in 1972 and expanded in the years 1978 to 1979 currently provides a maximum of about $1,800 annually to any student who pursues further education in any approved college or post-secondary institution.

Once again, the most disadvantaged among the adolescent group, those who have been expelled from high school or who have chosen to leave, as well as the many who are still on the student rolls but come from families that need their contribution to household expenses, cannot take advantage of the financial assistance that is available if they had full-time student status.

There are two ways to read the record outlined in the foregoing. On the one hand, significant new institutions and programs have contributed a great deal to facilitating the occupational development of young people. But with minor exceptions most of these innovations are available primarily or solely to those who have acquired a high school diploma. Those who cannot cope with the junior and senior high school curriculum or who are unable to learn useful skills from the college preparatory courses have had little opportunity to participate in the better vocational programs and the still rarer work-study programs currently available to only a very small percentage of all high school students. Moreover, in many areas the hard-to-employ will be excluded from enrolling in publicly supported post-secondary institutions that require a high school diploma for admission.

Despite the difficulties these nonacademic students confront because of their inability to negotiate the educational system, two limited but important innovations should be noted. 1) In the United States it is possible for those who have fallen off or left the regular educational track to acquire the equivalent of a high school diploma by passing an examination that entitles them to a General Educational Development (GED) Certificate. 2) Since the mid-1960s there have been a number of experiments, especially in some of the large cities with sizable minority populations, with alternative high schools. Some of these have had financial assistance and cooperation from local industries. One type of alternative school is a freestanding institution separate from and independent of the regular educational establishment. Another type, as in Philadelphia, was created by the educational authorities who designed, financed, and staffed it. In others, the local educational authority plays a role but the management is usually from the neighborhood.

Since the per annum costs of educating a pupil enrolled in a large city high school averages between $2,500 and $3,000, to start an alternative school and keep it in operation over a period of years is difficult. Moreover, evaluations show that only a minority of those enrolled stay long enough to earn a diploma and get a regular job or enter college.

The thrust of the foregoing review, which leads to the conclusion that those most in need of assistance receive the least attention and support, is correct only with regard to the educational system per se. When perspective is broadened to include the rubric of manpower programs, we find less neglect of the disadvantaged group than a purely educational focus would suggest.

As noted earlier, Congress acted in 1964 to help disadvantaged young people in several distinct ways: a summer youth program (Neighborhood Youth Corps), the Job Corps, and the inclusion of large numbers of young people in the regular manpower training efforts. There were earlier experimental programs, such as Mobilization for Youth in New York City. I will focus on the largest and most sustained efforts that came under the programs of the U.S. Department of Labor.

The Manpower Development and Training Act (MDTA) that Congress passed in the spring of 1962 initially carried a modest price tag, just over $50 million, to which the states were obliged to contribute. By 1978 the employment and training expenditures under the Comprehensive Employment and Training Act (CETA) approximated $11 billion.

The original purpose of MDTA was to assist skilled workers who had lost their jobs to get reemployed via participation in federally subsidized training programs, but young people were initially excluded from participating in these programs. In the next year, 1963, they could comprise 5% of the total enrollment. Attention to youth employment really began in 1964, when Congress initiated the Neighborhood Youth Corps (NYC) and Job Corps and agreed to the increased participation of young people in manpower training programs.

Without reviewing the evolution of these three efforts in the 13 years from 1964 until Congress passed the Youth Act of 1977, suffice it to say that Congress complicated the implementation of NYC by not appropriating funds until July 1 of each year. Since NYC was a summer employment program, it placed those responsible in an untenable position. Furthermore, those responsible for the design of NYC programs failed to integrate the summer program into programs designed to meet the needs of unemployed young people during the rest of the year, nor did Congress provide for monitoring the funds so they went to those most in need of assistance. For many years, many NYC summer jobs went to the relatives and friends of the local political power structure. But these serious drawbacks aside, Congress kept the program alive and over the years allocated more spaces and provided more dollars.

Initially training in the Job Corps was solely in residential centers, which meant that many inner-city youth were sent hundreds of miles from home for training, a transition that contributed to high turnover. In the early 1970s the Nixon Administration, which had little sympathy for any of the manpower programs it had inherited, would probably have liquidated the Job Corps program had it not been for George Shultz, former Secretary of Labor and then Secretary of the Treasury. Shultz kept the Job Corps alive by agreeing to cut back the number of residential centers, by opening day centers in the urban areas, and by reducing total enrollments by close to 50%. The Carter Administration, encouraged by the 1976 recommendation of the National Commission for Manpower Policy, asked for a doubling in the enrollment level, which Congress approved.

Reference was made earlier to the initial, implicit exclusion of youth from MDTA, followed by a 5% and later a 15% ceiling. After the mid-1960s all limitations were removed, with the result that the proportion of young people participating in different programs reached much higher levels; in some programs young people accounted for about half of all enrollees.

The following information on the participation of youth in these programs in fiscal year 1978 was drawn from the testimony of Assistant Secretary of Labor Ernest Green before the Subcommittee on Employment Opportunities of the Committee on Education and Labor of the House of Representatives in June of 1979:

Summer Youth Employment Program. Almost one million young people were enrolled in the program at a cost of $670 million. It was targeted to help low-income youth, and their earnings from participation in this program added one-fifth to the earned income of poverty families. It accounted for 80% of all the summer jobs that black youth obtained in contrast to 20% for white youth. Further, it raised the black youth employment to population ratio from one to three to three to five by virtue of participating in these governmental jobs.

Job Corps. Almost 29,000 were enrolled in June 1979 with an annual appropriation for this program of $235 million. Yearly participants numbered about 40,000. The enrollees are among the most disadvantaged—70% are members of minority groups; 87% are high school dropouts; half of those who enter the program read at or below the sixth-grade level. The recent evaluation by Mathematica is generally positive about this program in terms of post-Job Corps transitions into jobs, return to school, entrance into the armed forces, earnings, reduced crime, etc.

Comprehensive Employment and Training Act. During the period 1 October 1978 through 31 March 1979 young people under 22 years of age accounted for just under half of the 712,000 persons enrolled in work experience and training programs (Title I) and just under 20% of the almost 700,000 enrolled in public service jobs (Titles II and VI).

In March 1977 the Carter Administration obtained new legislation specifically focused on youth. The Youth Employment and Demonstration Projects Act of 1977 included four new programs: Young Adult Conservation Corps (YACC), Youth Incentive Entitlement Pilot Projects (YIEPP), Youth Community Conservation and Improvement Projects (YCCIP), and Youth Employment and Training Programs (YETP).

The major thrust of the first program, YACC, was to provide funds to the Departments of Agriculture and the Interior (30% of the total was allocated for state and local projects) for conservation efforts involving land and water. About 51,000 youth participated at a cost of $217 million during fiscal year 1979.

YIEPP received $222 million, to which local prime sponsors added another $90 million for the period January 1978 to June 1980, to undertake experimental and demonstration projects. The major effort is directed to a seven-site experiment that provides two months of summer employment and 20 weeks of employment or training at minimum wages during the rest of the school year for eligible low-income students in the project area who remain in or return to school. The major hypothesis to be tested is whether this program will reduce the number of dropouts and improve the postgraduation employment experience of the participants. An elaborate research effort under the direction of the Manpower Demonstration Research Corporation is being carried out with the assistance of Mathematica and Abt associates. In addition, there are demonstrations under way on a more modest scale in 10 other locations directed at improving some part of the school-to-work transition.

The third effort, YCCIP, is directed at out-of-school youth and aims to provide a significant employment experience for unemployed youth while improving the infrastructure of the community. The goal is to provide these young people not only with current income but with experience and skills that will enhance their later employability. In 1978 over 33,000 young people participated in this program, half of whom were black or Hispanic, and six of seven were economically disadvantaged. The budget for fiscal year 1979 was $107 million.

The last component of the Youth Act, YETP, is directed primarily at in-school youth between the ages of 14 and 21. It was the intent of Congress that the educational authorities be encouraged through a new appropriation to give more attention to improving the linkages between school and work. In March 1979, 174,000 students were receiving career employment experience, transition services, classroom or on-the-job training, or work experience.

With the exception of the YIEPP, which is being carefully monitored, it is questionable how much will be learned from this sizable effort about what works and what does not work, and for whom, because of the lack of a good management information system. Nevertheless, the scale of the various efforts is impressive, and many young people should profit from them. Secretary Green, in his concluding observations to his testimony, noted that 56% of the almost 2.5 million individuals served by all CETA programs will be young people under the age of 22.

To complete this assessment of Department of Labor programs facilitating the transition of young people into training and employment, brief reference should be made to the Job Service, the Bureau of Apprenticeship and Training, and the Targeted Jobs Tax Credit Program.

For many years the Job Service has provided labor market information and testing and counseling services to large numbers of in-school and out-of-school youth, but its major effort has been to assist those in search of employment. In fiscal year 1978 it placed over two million young people, almost 40% of whom were economically disadvantaged, in jobs that paid an average wage of $2.94 per hour. Many of these jobs were temporary and others were dead-end, but the sheer volume of placement is impressive.

The Bureau of Apprenticeship and Training (BAT) of the U.S. Department of Labor has been working with the Office of Youth Programs to bring the educational system into closer contact with apprenticeship programs through informational activities, part-time apprenticeship positions for high school seniors, and other activities aimed at establishing programs in emerging fields, such as computer programming and law enforcement, and in opening fields to women.

The Targeted Jobs Tax Credit Program, which is part of the Revenue Act of 1978 and for which the Employment Service has responsibility at state and local levels, provides liberal subsidies to employers who hire workers, including those below 24 years of age who are certified by the Job Service as "structurally unemployed." The financial benefits are substantial, but it remains to be seen whether they will suffice to overcome the bureaucratic inertia and employer disinclination to hire individuals whose competence, adaptability, and reliability are questionable. Nevertheless, in providing for such a liberal tax credit, Congress has demonstrated its good will; it has added yet another program to its efforts to facilitate the employment of hard-to-employ youths and adults.

I have now reviewed the many adaptations that were introduced into both the educational system and labor market institutions during the past two decades, many of which had as an objective improving the transition of young people from school to work. I will reserve until the last chapter my assessment of how well they succeeded and what still remains to be done to assure that fewer young people fall through the cracks.

Seven:
Improving the Transition

In this chapter I will summarize the more important findings that have emerged from this review of the developmental process through which young people pass from birth to adulthood, with particular focus on their transition from school to work. This analysis may prove useful as a guide to future policy interventions, particularly if we can develop a simple, but not simplistic, typology to help identify those young people likely to encounter trouble during their developmental years and to suggest the types of social intervention that might ease their transition.

Before discussing improved or new types of intervention, we will have to reach some judgment about the efficacy and efficiency of the large number of current programs that address the concerns of this monograph. Finally we will attempt to formulate a set of recommendations that hold some prospect of reducing the waste that now occurs as so many young people leave school and are unable to find jobs that provide the opportunity to acquire skills, that pay reasonable wages, and that offer the prospect to advance with time and experience.

While the primary focus of this chapter is on those groups of young people most likely to experience difficulty in making the transition from school to work, we must also take note of the ability of the economy to operate at or close to full employment; the requirements of the U.S. Department of Defense for military personnel for its active duty and reserve forces; the degree to which discrimination is likely to be lessened in the near future; the labor force trends including the large numbers of potential job seekers; and the other social, economic, and political forces that, for better or worse, will establish the framework within which improvements in the transition from school to work will be constrained.

The following are the important findings of earlier analyses that will provide the building blocks for a typology:

1. There is no persuasive evidence to support the contention that the U.S. economy has performed so poorly with respect to employment growth in general, and jobs for young people in particular, that the present level of youth unemployment is "a crisis." It is a fact that the unemployment levels for young people in their teens and early twenties are con-

siderably higher than they were in the early 1950s. It is also true, however, that the total number of young people who are employed is much higher. This last fact attests to the capacity of the economy to create additional jobs, since during the last quarter century, the numbers who reached working age have doubled.

2. A less favorable reading of the trends in youth employment and unemployment would result if we took note of the imbalances that exist between the number of young people still on the school rolls who would like a summer job or a part-time job during the months when school is in session but cannot find one. Since an early experience of work and of earning one's own spending money often contributes to maturity, the shortfall on this front may be dysfunctional.

3. When the focus is shifted from youth in general to minority youth, we find unequivocally that minority youth do face a job crisis that has existed since the end of economic expansion created by the Vietnam war, that is, since 1970. When we combine the young blacks and Hispanics who are not employed with those who are not looking for jobs because they see no prospect of finding one, we find that the unemployment level fluctuates at about 50%, and in some cities it is considerably higher. This is certainly a crisis.

4. One of the most deleterious consequences of racial discrimination is the resulting tendency to believe that all members of one group have undesirable traits and engage in undesirable behavior. Not all minority teenagers fail to make the transition from school to work. A significant minority of blacks, about 17%, move on from high school to junior or 4-year college. Another significant minority, especially those who have obtained their high school diplomas, find jobs in the civilian economy or apply to and are accepted into the armed forces. The most vulnerable are those who drop out or are pushed out of school prior to graduation, who have been truant for years, whose reading and other basic skills are at the sixth-grade level, and who live in families that have no connections with employers. These are the young people who comprise the crisis group.

5. There is a sizable group of white youngsters, from families in every income level, who also find the transition difficult. A large subgroup are those growing up in rural areas who must relocate to find work because the local economy has no place for them. Another significant number do not

graduate from high school; others are experimenting with drugs; some bolt because of conflicts with their parents and spend years wandering through the country or abroad; some start college and soon thereafter decide they cannot endure more studies and then spend months and often years moving in and out of jobs and relationships as they attempt to determine who they are and what they want to do. But most of this group are more fortunate than most minority teenagers. They are likely to have more education, to be more knowledgeable about the larger society and how it operates, to be able to get help from home in an emergency; and since they are white they are acceptable to employers if they seek a part- or full-time job.

On the basis of the foregoing we can tentatively present the following typology of the groups of young people during their transition from school to work.

The Straight Pattern. Those who make the transition with little or no difficulty because they have the qualifications that employers seek and have family support to draw on.

The Interrupted Pattern. Those who are unable or unwilling to move directly from school to work because they have not acquired the necessary credentials, because they are undergoing emotional turmoil, or because they are confused about their aims and goals. They need time to sort out their feelings, conflicts, and goals.

The Disturbed Pattern. Those who, because of poor preparation, alienation, minority status, or police records, are not acceptable to most employers and who find getting and holding a job unrewarding and frustrating. As an alternative this group often drifts into illicit activities.

The preparation of young people to assume adult roles is a responsibility shared by parents and those institutions that provide a wide range of services from preventive medicine to higher education. In most developed countries, institutions such as religious organizations, philanthropic institutions, and organizations serving young people, such as the Boy Scouts and Campfire Girls, often play an important role. But it is the family that has initial responsibility for nurturing during the early years of childhood, that is, until the youngster is ready to enter kindergarten or elementary school. In their comprehensive assessment of the role of the family in child rearing, Kenneth Keniston and his colleagues on the Carnegie Council on Children concluded that there are great discrepancies in the ability of families to meet their responsibilities as a result of differences in income, which translates into the goods and services they are able to provide their offspring, including such basics as food, housing, health care, education, access to mental health care, guidance, and recreation. Keniston's group concluded that the best way to assure that young people have a fair start in life is to provide all families with a basic level of income and access to essential public services.

The Keniston report was persuasive in demonstrating how many families, particularly those with a single head, are under such severe economic and other constraints that their children start life seriously handicapped when compared to those from families with average or above average income. The writers of the report did not analyze, however, the prospects of convincing the electorate to levy substantial additional taxes on themselves so that more money could be placed at the disposal of those with insufficient resources. Nor were they able to delineate the extent to which income transfers to disadvantaged families would lead to significant gains in the developmental experiences and the consequent later adjustment of their children.

Although money is rarely the complete answer, added income for disadvantaged families could ameliorate, if not neutralize, the following handicaps that characterize these families: the absence of one parent, usually the father; the emotional shortcomings of many parents as a result of poverty; physical disabilities present at birth or acquired in childhood; living quarters in urban slums where children are exposed to an oppressive environment from their earliest years; access only to poor schools and other inferior public services.

The Keniston report cited the gross inequalities among families despite our society's pretensions to "equality of opportunity," with which I agree, but I do not accept its proffered solutions. They are likely to fail on one of two grounds: 1) the public would not provide the additional income transfers that would be required to reduce, if not eliminate, these inequalities; 2) additional income alone would not neutralize the basic sources of the inequalities.

In the present context it may be helpful to consider briefly the scale of investments that American society is currently making available through its public sector for basic education, training, and subsidized employment opportunities for its young people. Any new proposals must be assessed with reference to these current efforts.

Without pretending to any sophisticated calculations, we can state that a family in a large urban community outside of the South, whose child attends nursery school, Head Start or kindergarten for two years, and the public school system for 12 years, has had access to educational services that at present levels cost an average of $30,000. If the young person belongs to a low-income family and has participated in federally subsidized summer employment programs for two years, spends one year in one of the new programs established for out-of-school youth and an additional year on a public service job, he or she has had access to another $10,000 of training and employment opportunities provided by the federal government. Hence, the public sector currently invests about $40,000 for the education and training of young persons to help them obtain the prerequisites for employment.

Many of those who fall into the "disturbed pattern" have been the recipients directly or indirectly of much larger public expenditures. Consider those who grow up in a family that has been on the welfare rolls for some or all of the years of their childhood and adolescence. Consider further those who broke the law and were sent to a reformatory for a year or two, and when they were released became drug addicts, which later led to their entering a detoxification program where they received treatment for a period of six months to a year. This listing, which does not exhaust the amount of public money that may be expended on children in families that are intermittently or regularly dependent on welfare, can easily result in the outlay of another $40,000 prior to the young person's reaching 18 or 20 years of age.

The point of this exercise in arithmetic is neither to present careful estimates nor to suggest that the total of between $40,000 and $80,000 of public expenditures per child is evidence of a compassionate society's determination to provide all young people with a fair start. The Keniston report is a powerful reminder of how far this society falls short of achieving that goal. But it does force us to consider with a critical eye the scale, scope, and potential for any new proposals advanced to improve the transition of young people from school to work.

Before reviewing the societal interventions that have been introduced to improve the prospects of young people to function effectively in the adult world, let us consider briefly the macrofactors, other than public expenditures, that will have an impact on present and future policies and programs. While

we can accept the validity of the contention that our young
people are the nation's future, we cannot ignore the other
realities and expenditures that command the public's attention
and allegiance.

Few economists believe that the employment problems of
disadvantaged young people can be resolved unless our
economy can be made to run at, or close to, full employment,
not for a year or so but for a long stretch of time. In mid-1979
when the Secretary of Labor stated that, in the face of the new
OPEC price for oil, it would prove difficult to prevent the overall unemployment rate from rising to 6.5% or higher in 1980 (It
actually reached closer to 8% by the summer of 1980), we are
reminded of how far we are from the full employment objectives of the Humphrey-Hawkins Act of 1978. When we add to
this the disquieting fact that the economy was operating at
double digit inflation and by the spring of 1980 was in a recession, the employment preconditions for "solving" or even substantially moderating the job and career problems of disadvantaged young people had become exceedingly difficult, if not
impossible, to achieve in the near term. This does not mean of
course that nothing should be ventured or that nothing will
succeed; it means that any efforts undertaken must confront
an unfavorable national economic and employment outlook.

Since its involvement in World War II, American society
has used the law and administrative policies to reduce racism
and discrimination that have been part of the nation's experience from its beginning. From one perspective, the changes
that have occurred have been substantial, even remarkable.
But from another perspective we might ask: To what extent
does racism and discrimination still harm, cripple, and destroy
the aspirations and potential of the sizable number of our
black and Hispanic families and their offspring? The only
possible answer is that the toll continues to be immense, a
fact that even sympathetic whites often fail to understand or
acknowledge as they form their attitudes and shape their
behavior with respect to matters of race.

That substantial discriminatory barriers are still in place
is clear from the conditions under which many young black
persons are being reared today and under which others will
be reared tomorrow. This is pointed up by the facts that only
about one in two black youngsters who reach 18 have been
reared by both their natural parents; that close to the same
proportion are brought up in families at or close to the poverty

level; that a much higher proportion are born into families that live in ghetto areas and attend schools that are largely or totally segregated.

⚹ The enumeration of these conditions should suffice to warn even the most optimistic social reformers that even if the American people decide to make a special effort, as the late Whitney Young suggested, to alleviate and eliminate these pathologies as reparations for past wrongs or in recognition that such an effort would contribute to the stability and welfare of the body politic, even then it would take another generation or two, as Martin Luther King perceived, to eliminate most of the evils of discrimination that are still present.

⚹ The third macro-constraint to alleviating youth unemployment are those members of the society, present and future, who will be competing for the new jobs that will open up. Putting aside for the moment the adult members of the work force who are temporarily unemployed or underemployed, we must take into consideration the large numbers of women, older persons, and immigrants, legal or undocumented, who will compete directly or indirectly with young people for available jobs. Although women account for more than half of all the additions to the labor force since the end of World War II, many more millions are in the wings ready to accept part- or full-time employment when new jobs become available.

While participation in the work force of persons above 55 years of age has been dropping precipitously over the last several decades, recent federal and state legislative actions that eliminate some or all of the provisions for compulsory retirement based on age is a sign that some, probably many, older persons are interested in prolonging their stay in the labor force. The high level of inflation, and its probable persistence, must be seen as a factor forcing many to delay withdrawing from the labor force, for only if they continue to work can they protect their standard of living.

Finally, few of the American public realize that legal immigrants contribute approximately 12% to the annual growth of the labor force and that a conservative allowance for undocumented workers would lead to a doubling of that percentage. Given their circumstances and alternatives, immigrants are likely to be eager workers, willing to accept conditions that would repel some young persons and discourage others.

⚹ In sum, the constant shortfall of the U.S. economy from full employment, the continued pervasiveness of racism and discrimination, and the large numbers of present and potential competitors for jobs point to the difficulties of formulating policies aimed at ameliorating and solving the employment problems of disadvantaged young people. But still a responsible democracy must make the effort, an even greater effort in the face of these obstacles, to provide work for disadvantaged young people.

Let us now look briefly at the principal intervention programs that have been tried, particularly the new ones established since the Great Society programs were introduced in the mid-1960s.

Over the past several decades most of the states have adopted school equalization formulas to provide a common funding base, since the local tax base can vary so much from community to community within a state. Recently, the courts have been encouraging state legislators to take even more direct action toward equalization of educational expenditures. In 1965, with the passage of the Elementary and Secondary Education Act, the federal government started to make funds available to school districts with disproportionately large numbers of students from low-income homes.

Even with the efforts at equalization of expenditures, most disadvantaged children have not been able to keep abreast of those from middle-income families who attend suburban schools. The single criterion of financial equalization may be inappropriate for assessing whether or not federal funds provide equal educational opportunity. Disadvantaged children may be helped by these extra funds, which translate into extra services for them, but they may still lag far behind their more fortunately situated peers.

The critical finding is that, despite state and federal efforts aimed at equalization, a disproportionate number of children from low-income homes fail to acquire the basic competencies in reading, writing, and mathematics. Many of them test at several years below the norm in most or all subjects. There is ground for debating whether employer requirements are excessive, but it is hard to argue with the contention that, in an increasingly technological society, sixth-grade reading and computational skills are hardly adequate for the employability of such young people.

There is no sense in trying to apportion blame for these educational failures on parents, the young persons themselves, or the school system. The incontrovertible fact that must be acknowledged is that the school does not provide a useful educational experience for a great many young people, and this failure of the schools adds immeasurably to the problems of these young people in making a satisfactory transition to the world of work.

With respect to vocational training at the high school level, we find that, for the most part, there is little to commend it; and it offers even less to students who are having difficulty coping with the regular curriculum. This is not to say that the vocational preparatory route would not be desirable for many of these students, particularly if the programs were well structured and staffed. But since the economy is rapidly moving toward white-collar work, most prospective workers need to acquire basic competencies in reading, communications, and mathematics. A curriculum that does not teach these basic competencies is failing.

The substantial state, local, and private expenditures for community colleges and for the expansion of state universities in urban centers, which serve a large number of young people from low-income families, did indeed broaden their opportunities to acquire technical skills and/or degrees that facilitate their later employment. But these significant gains did little for those most in need of assistance, those who found high school so disappointing and unrewarding that they dropped out.

※ In the last two decades the federal government's training programs have been increasingly directed to serving those who are encountering difficulties in the labor market. With the exception of the Job Corps, which never served more than 50,000 young people during the course of a year, there has been little training directed toward skill acquisition that could lead to good paying jobs. Most other federal programs exposed young people to some work experience, little more. Summer youth programs, for example, were essentially a means of putting money in the hands of needy young people.

In my view, the federal training programs enabled very few young people to obtain a mastery of skills that would enable them to obtain regular jobs with prospects of advancement. At most, it provided them with some work experience and socialization in the work place, a useful but insufficient increment to their employability.

※ The following are usually considered to comprise transition services: testing, guidance, counseling, labor market information, placement, support services (child care, etc.). In my opinion, school-based occupational guidance is a weak reed, especially for disadvantaged young people because of the limited knowledge of many counselors about the changing realities of the labor market and their biased views of the options open to minority youth. Many other guidance and counseling efforts, in school and out of school, also have limited value because they are not linked directly to job placement, which is what most young people need and want when they seek assistance in finding jobs. Many young people do not have the experience or the self-confidence to know how to use labor market information in finding a job for themselves. What they really need is specific help in locating a job.

While Job Service is often unable to meet the needs of hard-to-employ adults and young people because of the relatively small number of attractive job openings it has available and because of the pressures that employers exert to be sent only strong candidates, the fact remains that many young people do get jobs through the employment service.

Perhaps the most difficult transition services to provide are those required by young workers to make them job-ready; for example, young women who cannot accept a job unless they can make child-care arrangements during the hours they are at work. Satisfactory child-care arrangements are difficult to find and often cost so much that it does not pay the prospective worker to take a job.

Another type of supportive service needed by many prospective workers is some type of therapeutic or rehabilitative health care (from a hernia operation to eye glasses). Liaison between the employment service and the local health agencies is so loose in many areas that young people who need medical intervention to make them job-ready frequently cannot obtain it.

If we compare the quantity and quality of transition services available to young people in the late 1970s with the early 1960s we can read the record in two ways. On the one hand, there has been a substantial improvement in the number and quality of such services as job banks in the employment service that list available openings and publicly supported child-care facilities for low-income mothers. On the other hand, most disadvantaged young people who lack skills, experience, connections, and self-confidence are still unable to develop a successful linkage to the world of work. In the final analysis, transition services that are not directly linked to jobs are not likely to be helpful, particularly for those who are having the most difficulty in finding jobs.

Improving the Transition

In 1971, with the enactment of the Emergency Employment Act, the federal government re-entered the arena of direct job creation for the unemployed and the underemployed for the first time since the 1930s. It started with a modest two-year program with an appropriation of $2.2 billion; as a result, 226,000 persons obtained jobs during the fiscal year 1972. With the establishment of CETA in 1973 and with its reauthorization in 1978, the involvement of the federal government in direct Public Service Employment (PSE) for the chronically unemployed, as well as for victims of the downward business cycle, resulted in 725,000 jobs by 1978.

It was noted earlier that less than one out of five PSE jobs has gone to young people, although they account for approximately half of all the unemployed. One reason for this discrepancy is that the federal programs were specifically aimed at helping regular workers who had lost their jobs during the 1974 recession. Moreoever, the considerably higher earnings that come with PSE jobs have led the prime sponsors to reserve them, for the most part, for heads-of-households whose income needs are greater. Finally, many PSE positions require workers with some demonstrated competence and work experience. For all of these reasons, we find that direct job creation by the federal government has served relatively small numbers of young people. Furthermore, we know that many who have had a PSE job have not done well when it came time to make a transition into a regular job in the public or private economy. This remains one of the serious limitations of the PSE progam.

We know that the sizable increases in local, state, and federal expenditures for education, training, transition services, and employment during the past several decades resulted in substantial gains for many young people in their preparation for the world of work. But, as we have seen, these enlarged expenditures made only a marginal impact on improving the employability and employment of the sizable minority who were encountering difficulties in the regular school system. They dropped out without having acquired the competencies needed to get and hold regular jobs. The federal manpower programs gave these young people a second chance, but only a minority, probably one in three, received the training, transition services, and/or job experience that helped them to make a permanent attachment to the labor market.

From this analysis of the principal institutions and processes involved in the transition of young people from school to work, my principal conclusions and recommendations follow:

1. The process of transition works relatively satisfactorily for most young people and there is no need for major public interventions. Family and friends are able to help most young people obtain a job once they are ready to enter the labor market.

2. The transition is difficult for high school dropouts who have failed to acquire the basic competencies to perform white-collar work in an increasingly service-oriented economy. Some never make an effective adjustment to the world of work. When these young people who belong to minority groups have trouble with the law and are alienated from society, their job problems are further compounded.

3. The variety of societal interventions, specifically those directed to improving the effectiveness of the educational process and to the provision of second-chance opportunities via manpower training and related programs, have had positive outcomes for only a minority of the young people who need special assistance to find and hold jobs.

4. There is no prospect of our society's being able or willing to design the supportive programs that low-income, particularly minority, families with female heads living in slum conditions require for a more conducive environment in which to rear their children. We have made some progress toward alleviating these unfortunate conditions and we will, it is hoped, make more. But the handicaps to children born into and reared in such families are great and will not soon be removed.

5. These children require schools where curricula, teaching methods, and reinforcement devices assure that almost all of them will be able to acquire the basic competencies they will need to hold jobs when they are ready to start work. When the schools fail, these young people need second-chance institutions that will enable them to acquire the competencies they failed to master within the school system.

The assumption that more public expenditures are needed to accomplish the foregoing is not convincing. The current amount spent for public education and for federal manpower programs is substantial, and there is little to support the presumption that simply more money will result in a significant improvement in outcomes for the young people most in need of help.

In light of these findings, what should be done? Only a cynic would suggest that we leave the situation alone and wait for time to work a cure. Each year, 800,000 or so young people reach working age inadequately prepared for work and the responsibilities of adulthood. Approximately half of them are minority youth, blacks or Hispanics. After several years of hanging around street corners, moving in and out of short-term jobs, hustling, or enrolling in government programs, possibly half of these poorly qualified young people have not made a definitive attachment to the labor force by the age of 24. They are, and most will remain, marginal workers.

Helping these young people to achieve an acceptable level of competency so they can compete for white-collar jobs is one goal; helping them to obtain access to the jobs that open up is another. They cannot be left to make their own way. They need assistance in effecting a linkage to the world of work. Accordingly, every possible avenue should be explored—from political pressures that hold school boards accountable to specialized training for principals and teachers in ghetto schools—to improve the level of achievement of the young people who attend these schools. Tighter discipline, modified curricula, remedial services are needed and can help. But the apathy and alienation of these students must also be countered. Nobody can learn unless he or she becomes engaged and puts forth the requisite effort.

Many ghetto youngsters are indifferent to whether they attend classes, listen to the teacher, or do their homework. They believe that the society is rigged against them; they will never have a fair chance. No school, on its own, can overcome such pessimism and alienation. Our society must establish explicit contracts with these young people from their fourteenth year or preferably earlier that might go as follows: Those who pass all of their subjects will have first claim on summer jobs; those who perform well on their summer jobs will have a guarantee of part-time work during the school year; those who complete high school will be assured of a job or a place in junior or 4-year college; those who encounter difficulty with their studies will have the opportunity to obtain remedial education after school hours and on Saturday. The theme would not vary; opportunities would be available to all who demonstrate that they are willing to take advantage of them.

One must quickly admit that the foregoing proposal could result in "creaming," whereby those young people who demonstrate a willingness to make an effort on their own behalf will be rewarded. But as long as opportunities remain open for those who do not initially respond or who are unable to meet the standards, no serious inequity will result. Society cannot help those who are unwilling to help themselves.

Acquiring the basic competencies for the transition to work, with or without the assistance of the contractual model sketched above, is only one blade of the scissors. The other is that an adequate number of job openings, apprenticeships, military service, or other opportunities be made available in the form of "reserved places" for all the young people who have kept their part of the bargain. The three levels of government, by far the largest employer in the country accounting for approximately one out of every five jobs, must assume a leading role. But the participation of the private sector is equally essential. Although the private sector, responding to President Johnson's appeal, made some contribution to alleviating the employment problems of the hard-to-employ in the late 1960s, it has not continued to play an active role. Leadership at the local level will need to involve the heads of business organizations both large and small and the trade unions to provide the job openings and establish the linkages needed to direct qualified young persons who would otherwise not make it past the hiring gate.

If the federal funds currently available for young people were reprogrammed, they would probably be sufficient, or nearly so, to support both the in-school and out-of-school efforts that have just been outlined. The real challenge is to impress on the American people, and particularly on local employers and trade unions, that without their cooperation and active participation, millions of young people will be consigned to live as outcasts, unable to work at regular jobs that provide reasonable rewards and reasonable prospects of advancement.

A society that fails to live up to its principle of equality of opportunity and fails to address the plight of those denied opportunity incurs high costs in human denigration, lost output, crime, and welfare; and thereby adds to its vulnerability, now and in the future. If it is responsive, it may not fully succeed; but if it fails to make the effort, it cannot respect itself or command the respect of others.

Suggested Reading

Adams, Arvil V., and Mangum, Garth L. *The Lingering Crisis of Youth Unemployment.* (W.E. Upjohn Institute, 1978).

Anderson, Bernard E., and Sawhill, Isabel V., eds. *Youth Employment and Public Policy.* The American Assembly on Youth Employment, Arden House. (Englewood Cliffs, N.J.: Prentice-Hall, 1980).

Brimmer, Andrew. *The Economic Position of Black Americans.* (National Commission for Manpower Policy, Special Report No. 9, July, 1976).

DeLone, Richard H. *Small Futures.* The Carnegie Council on Children. (New York: Harcourt Brace Jovanovich, Inc., 1979)

Gabriel, Richard A. *Crisis in Command.* (New York: Hill & Wang, 1978).

Ginzberg, Eli and Bray, Douglas W. *The Uneducated.* (New York: Columbia University Press, 1953).

Ginzberg, Eli, et al. *The Negro Potential.* (New York: Columbia University Press, 1956).

Ginzberg, Eli, ed. *Values and Ideals of American Youth.* (New York: Columbia University Press, 1961).

Ginzberg, Eli. *Good Jobs, Bad Jobs, No Jobs.* (Cambridge, Mass.: Harvard University Press, 1979).

Ginzberg, Eli, ed. *Employing the Unemployed.* (New York: Basic Books, 1980).

Ginzberg, Eli, et al. *Tell Me About Your School.* (National Commission for Employment Policy, 1980).

Keniston, Kenneth. *All Our Children: The American Family Under Pressure.* Report for the Carnegie Council on Children. (New York: Harcourt Brace Jovanovich, Inc., 1977).

Levitan, Sar E., et al. *Counting the Labor Force.* (Final Report of the National Commission on Employment and Unemployment Statistics, 1979).

Moynihan, Daniel and Glazer, Nathan. *Beyond the Melting Pot.* (Cambridge, Mass.:The MIT Press, 1963).

National Commission for Employment Policy. *Expanding Employment Opportunities for Disadvantaged Youth.* Fifth Annual Report, 1980.

Reder, Melvin. "Human Capital and Economic Discrimination," in *Human Resources and Economic Welfare.* Essays in Honor of Eli Ginzberg, ed. by Ivar Berg. (New York: Columbia University Press, 1972).

Statistical Abstract of the United States. 1978.

Thernstrom, Stephan. *Poverty and Progress: Social Mobility in a Nineteenth Century City.* (Cambridge, Mass.: Harvard University Press, 1964).